THE **NEW BEST** OF **FINE WOODWORKING**

Building
Small Projects

Building
Small Projects

The Editors of
Fine Woodworking

The Taunton Press

The Taunton Press
Inspiration for hands-on living®

The Taunton Press, Inc., 63 South Main Street, PO Box 5506, Newtown, CT 06470-5506
e-mail: tp@taunton.com

Distributed by Publishers Group West

Jacket/Cover design: Susan Fazekas
Interior design: Susan Fazekas
Layout: Susan Lampe-Wilson
Front Cover Photographer: Asa Christiana
Back Cover Photographers: Asa Christiana, Michael Pekovich, Strother Purdy

The New Best of Fine Woodworking® is a trademark of The Taunton Press, Inc.,
registered in the U.S. Patent and Trademark Office.

Library of Congress Cataloging-in-Publication Data

Building small projects / the editors of Fine woodworking.
     p. cm. -- (The new best of Fine woodworking)
ISBN-13: 978-1-56158-730-8
ISBN-10: 1-56158-730-3
  1. Woodwork--Amateurs' manuals. 2. House furnishings--Amateurs' manuals. I. Fine woodworking.
II. Series.
  TT185.B783 2004
  684'.08--dc22

                              2004006984
Printed in the United States of America
10 9 8 7 6 5 4 3

The following manufacturers/names appearing in *Building Small Projects* are trademarks:
3M®, Brusso®, Dremel®, Harris®, Leigh®, Masonite®, Morse®, Scotch-Brite®, Stanley®, Titebond®,
Varathane®, Watco®, Waterlox®

Working wood is inherently dangerous. Using hand or power tools improperly or ignoring safety
practices can lead to permanent injury or even death. Don't try to perform operations you learn about
here (or elsewhere) unless you're certain they are safe for you. If something about an operation doesn't
feel right, don't do it. Look for another way. We want you to enjoy the craft, so please keep safety
foremost in your mind whenever you're in the shop.

Acknowledgments

Special thanks to the authors, editors, art directors, copy editors, and other staff members of *Fine Woodworking* who contributed to the development of the articles in this book.

Contents

Introduction

The first useful object I ever built out of wood was a lidded box. It was not a piece to admire for its beauty —but I was thrilled that all the parts simply fit together. I was only 12, and I built the box without supervision and completed it with all 10 digits intact, something that no doubt thrilled my parents. The box was made of materials I had picked up at a home construction site—plywood and wood screws. As far as I knew at the time, I invented the joinery: butt joints reinforced with glue and screws.

I slathered several coats of paint over the piece and added a hasp and lock to guard my not-so-rare coin collection and a few risqué post cards of Atlantic City bathing beauties. The box survives to this day, intact, the treasures of the time long since swapped for a place to store a few seldom-used tools.

I can't say that my plywood box project was the experience that inspired me to eventually pick up woodworking in my adult years, but the process of building it brought a sense of satisfaction no different from what I feel today upon completing a piece.

By calling these projects small, we don't mean to imply simple or uninspired. The projects we have chosen—boxes, cabinets, tables, stools—run the gamut from simple

to elaborate. Some may be completed in a weekend; others may take months. They are taken from the pages of *Fine Woodworking* magazine and come with detailed instructions to walk you through the process, step by step.

Depending on your skill level, you may want to dive right in and tackle the classic Thomas Jefferson's Writing Desk, a challenging yet rewarding project. Or maybe you want something to do in an afternoon —check out the plans for Shaker Oval Boxes. No matter what you make, remember to have fun. It's not just about the object; let the process itself be an adventure.

—Anatole Burkin,
Editor of *Fine Woodworking*

A Small Elegant Box

BY GARY ROGOWSKI

Simplicity in design is often mistaken for having a simple mind or a lack of ideas. Accuse me of this innocence, but I still prefer shapes to be more modest than bold. Because of this inclination, I've always found Japanese design to be inspiring, especially traditional designs for packaging. When I wanted a new joinery project for students attending my woodworking school, I recalled a bamboo sushi container made with simple lap joints. I changed the design to use alder instead of bamboo and to include a bottom lined with rice paper. I left out the fish.

The first step in this project is to decide on the proportions of the box. It's surprising how different a box looks when you change the proportions from, say, 2:1 to 5:2 and to 8:5 (the classic golden mean). Try some basic outlines on a piece of paper to see the difference. Then mill up some stock ½ in. thick and 2 in. wide.

Lay out the lap joints at half the height of the stock (1 in. in this case) and mark

Pinned lap joints and shaped sides refine a basic design.

A SIMPLE BOX WITH A DELICATE TOUCH

The ideas for small boxes come from many sources. This box made of alder wood is based on a traditional sushi container from Japan. It uses lap joints, brass pins, and carefully rounded sides to achieve its effect.

End grain on lid is textured with a gouge.

Rabbet on lid, ⅛ in. x ½ in.

Lid, ½ in. x 4 in. x 10 in.

Rabbet, ³⁄₁₆ in. x ⁵⁄₁₆ in., accepts bottom.

Brass pins, 1⅛ in., reinforce the lap joints.

Box is built from ½-in.-thick stock. Sides are rounded after assembly.

2 in.

½ in.

⁵⁄₁₆ in.

⅛ in.   ³⁄₁₆ in.

Ebony handle, ³⁄₁₆ in. x ¼ in. x 1¾ in.

Rice paper is glued to box bottom with polyurethane finish.

Box bottom, ¼-in. birch plywood, 3⅜ in. x 9⅜ in.

Fingerhold cutout, 1¼ in. dia.

Mortises accept handle.

Brass pins, 1¼ in., hold the bottom in place.

Handle

2 in.

4 in.

10 in.

Cut Lap Joints and Rabbets

Pull out your tablesaw and dado blade, if you must, but lap joints and rabbets are just as easily cut with a good dovetail saw and a paring chisel. Just remember that these simple joints have very little gluing surface, so they must fit well to gain any strength from the joint. For added strength, I reinforce the joints with 1⅛-in. brass pins after glue-up.

The rabbets to accept the bottom are easily cut on a router table. Because I built the box with staggered joints, I cut the ³⁄₁₆-in. by ³⁄₁₆-in. rabbets for the bottom into each piece, with a stopped cut at the finger end and a through-cut at the other. End these stopped cuts well in from the end so that you lessen the chances of blowing out the short grain on the sides. The rabbets are squared up with a chisel before the box is assembled. Though this is a small box, glue-up takes more clamps than you might imagine. Make sure that pressure is evenly distributed and that everything is square, then leave it clamped up overnight.

Shape the Sides with a Handplane

The next day, round the sides of the box with a sharp plane—I use either a low-angle block plane or a #3 smoothing plane (see the top photo on the facing page). Because you're planing end grain, work in from the corner, even if it means planing against the long grain. You can clean up any tearout by carefully planing in the proper direction once the bulk of the shaping has been completed.

Draw pencil marks around the edges so you can gauge how far in you want to shape. I round in about one third of the thickness of the stock, leaving the middle of the box sides the full ½ in. thick. Be careful at the bottom edges because too much shaping will weaken the wall covering up the rabbet.

Start to round out near the edges of the sides first and work your way back toward

them with a square. Then lay out the depth of cut with a marking gauge set to cut just less than the thickness of the stock. Cutting the depth of the fingers to just less than the thickness of the stock enables you to clamp up right over the joint, making it much easier to glue up. The long grain rather than the end grain will be left proud so that it won't get in the way of your clamp pad.

When it comes to arranging the lap joints at each corner, you can stagger the fingers around the box: For this box I placed one upper finger and one lower finger on each side piece, which looks good to me. Or you can cut both fingers on the upper or lower half of each side. It's up to you, but bear in mind that when you stagger the joints, it's a much tougher glue-up. Any clamping pressure on the sides tends to collapse them in toward each other, so it helps to glue up the box with the bottom in place to act as a spacer. The easier method aligns the sockets and fingers opposite each other so that each side is held in place by the other when pressure is applied.

Box Building with Lap Joints and Rabbets

LAY OUT THE LAP JOINTS. To lay out the fingers, use a marking gauge set to just less than the stock thickness.

MAKE THE FIRST CUT. Use a dovetail saw to cut a kerf at half the width of the stock.

FOLLOW THE CHISELED LINE. Establish a shoulder line using a paring chisel and cut away the excess.

CLEAN UP WITH A CHISEL. Square up the joint with a paring chisel.

MARK FROM THE JOINT, NOT FROM A RULER. With one shoulder cut, lay out the mating lap joint directly from the stock.

STOPPED RABBETS ON THE ROUTER TABLE. Using a straight bit and stop block (not shown) on the router table, cut a rabbet in the bottom of the sides—be careful not to blow out the end grain. Use a paring chisel to square up the corners of the rabbets.

AN ARMY OF CLAMPS. Af- ter a dry run with the clamps, lay out the pieces and apply glue to the fingers and shoulders. Add clamps one by one, and check frequently to make sure the box stays square and that every joint closes.

Shaping the Box

Rounding the sides. A small block plane cuts in across the end grain. First, a bevel is established, then the entire side is rounded to a fair curve. A pencil line prevents mistakes by showing how much of the stock should be planed away at the edges of the box.

SHAPING THE TOP. The author uses a bench hook and a block plane (above) to round the top to a fair curve.

the middle until you get a nicely rounded shape. Finish up the shaping with a newly honed blade set for a very fine shaving, and be careful of any potential end-grain problems.

Shape the Lid and Handle

The lid is cut out exactly the same size as the overall dimensions of the box before being shaped. Once the box sides have been shaped, the box lid will overhang the sides nicely. Rabbet the lid on the router table so that it fits just inside the box. Place the lid over the edge of a bench hook and clamp it so that you can round it with your plane.

Again, use a pencil line to gauge how far to round the lid. After shaping, carve the end grain of the lid with a gouge (I use a #3) for an attractive bit of texture.

Before shaping the lid, drill a 1¼-in. fingerhold in the center of the lid and rout grooves to accept a handle. I use a ³⁄₁₆-in. straight bit in my router table to make these stopped cuts. Chisel them out square and fit a contrasting wood as the handle. I used ebony as the handle for this alder box and left it a bit tall in the grooves. I make the same box out of walnut and use holly for the handle. It helps to do all of your staining before gluing the handle in place.

Add Details to Refine the Box

There are a couple of other details I add to this simple box. I glue rice paper to the bottom using a water-based polyurethane finish from Varathane as the glue (see the photo above). I put the finish on the bottom and the oversized rice paper, then press them together. No clamping is required. When dry, trim the rice paper exactly to size. The bottom sits in the rabbets and is nailed in place with brass pins. I use a slightly longer pin to nail each of the lap joints. Such thin stock has a tendency to split, so predrill the holes for the pins with an undersized bit. Then carefully tap in the pins, protecting the underside of the box with a towel or a scrap piece of carpet.

This alder box is bleached to give it a bone-white look. I use a couple of coats of a commercial two-part bleaching solution. After bleaching, I clean the wood with a water-dampened rag. The walnut boxes I make are ebonized using a stain made up of white vinegar and a piece of old steel wool. I give the solution a few days to mix up, strain out the steel wool particles and then wipe this stain onto the walnut with a rag. The amount of darkening that occurs will depend upon the tannin in the walnut, and at this stage it can look a little drab. But as soon as you put a clear coat over it, the beauty of the stained walnut really pops. I pad on a few coats of clear blond shellac as a final touch to this very simple design.

GARY ROGOWSKI runs the Northwest Woodworking Studio in Portland, Ore., and is a contributing editor to *Fine Woodworking* magazine.

Making Mitered Boxes

BY GARY ROGOWSKI

If a dovetailed box speaks volumes about your craftsmanship, what can a simple mitered box say? From a practical view, mitered joints require only a quick setup on the tablesaw, and once set up, the cuts are repeatable; a mitered box says that you're frugal with your time. From an artistic view, mitered joints are beautiful, with only long grain showing around the sides of the box. Because mitered joints need strengthening, you have to add splines or keys, but these can impart a distinctive and elegant flavor to your design. So, in the end, a mitered box also can speak well about the level of your craftsmanship.

To achieve continuous grain on a box, resaw the parts from thick stock (see the facing page). For a four-sided box, cut carcase miters on the tablesaw with the blade tipped to 45°. Use a miter gauge or a dedicated crosscut jig for these cuts. Don't use a standard crosscut jig for your angled cuts or you'll end up with a gaping hole in the

middle of the jig. Make a pair of practice cuts on scrapwood and check the results with a combination square.

When making the cut on the second end of each side, be sure to use a stop on the jig to ensure that your cuts are made exactly to length. If you need to make minor adjustments or clean up a rough sawcut, use a tuned and sharpened handplane. I use a low-angle block plane because it cuts end grain effortlessly.

Assemble and Glue Up the Boxes

All but the smallest of carcase miters need strengthening. The mitered joint is actually a cross between long grain and end grain, so it's not the most optimal gluing surface. You can strengthen a joint either before or after the box has been assembled. In either case, assembling a box miter requires planning. Lay out and practice your clamping system before applying glue. Some finessing always is required to get the pressure in exactly the right spots.

Resawing for Continuous Grain

Sides resawn from thick stock on the bandsaw will produce a box with four matching corners.

Flipping over the resawn stock gives the outside of the box two corners of continuous grain and two corners of book-matched grain.

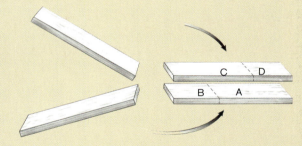

Before cutting the miters, label each side of the box so that the corners match up.

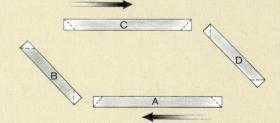

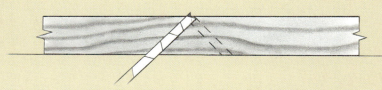

To minimize the gap in the grain caused by the miter cuts, set the blade height on the tablesaw to barely clear the top, or outside, face of the stock.

Two Methods of Strengthening a Joint Before Assembly

Reinforcing a miter joint with a concealed biscuit or a through-spline aids assembly by aligning the sides during gluing.

Biscuits

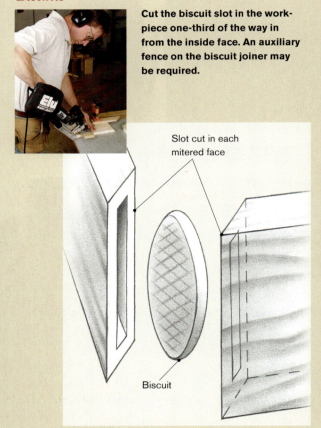

Cut the biscuit slot in the workpiece one-third of the way in from the inside face. An auxiliary fence on the biscuit joiner may be required.

Slot cut in each mitered face

Biscuit

Splines

When cutting splined miters on the tablesaw, set the blade and fence to make the spline cut in the thickest part of the workpiece.

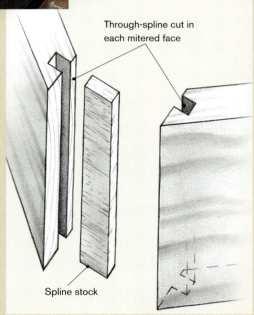

Through-spline cut in each mitered face

Spline stock

Band clamps work well if they don't have to apply excessive pressure. Inaccurately cut joints will not pull together with band clamps, but well-cut joints will snug right up with just one or two band clamps. Masking tape also can provide light clamping pressure suitable for smaller boxes. Wrap a dry-assembled box with masking tape across the width of each of the miter joints. Then slice open one joint, lay out the box flat and apply glue to the joints. Fold the box back together and retape that last joint.

Whatever kind of strengthening you employ, it is a good idea to size the mitered end of each piece of wood before assembling the box. Wipe a thin layer of glue across the end grain and, before it has dried hard, scrape off the excess glue. Now the porous end grain won't suck up the glue and weaken the joint when you're ready for final assembly.

Strengthen Miters Before You Assemble the Box

The two simplest ways to strengthen the miter joints are to add biscuits or through-splines before gluing up the box. Because you cut them in the length of the joint, the sides of the box still show only long grain, and the biscuits and splines help align the joints during glue-up.

Biscuited miters provide unseen strength–With the miters cut and trimmed exactly to length, set the biscuit-joiner fence at 45° and adjust for the proper depth of cut. Make the cuts about one-third in from the inside edge to use the greatest depth of wood. If your biscuit joiner won't make a cut this close to the fence, attach a block of wood to the fence with double-sided tape. Mark the center of the cut or cuts on the inside face of the stock, clamp the board securely, and make the cuts.

Through-splined miters are strong and decorative–The easiest method of cutting through-splines is to use the table-saw. With the blade already angled 45° from the miter cut, make the spline groove using a miter gauge and the saw fence. Set the blade height carefully and set the fence so that the groove is cut about two-thirds back from the outside corner. This makes for a longer and stronger spline. If available, use a flat-tooth blade for a square-bottom groove.

For an interesting design detail, I like to make up spline stock from a contrasting wood. When doing so, it's important that the grain runs in the same direction as the box sides so that all of the parts shrink and expand in unison, but this is also the strongest orientation for the splines. Rough out the stock on the bandsaw as wide as you need it and close to thickness. Make the stock long enough to easily hang on to, and trim it to thickness as if it were a tenon, using a tenoning jig or holder to

Miter and Glue Up the Box

KEEP A CARRIAGE JIG EXCLUSIVELY FOR CUTTING MITERS. Use a stop block when cutting the second miter to ensure matching parts are cut to the same lengths.

PREPARATIONS MAKE PERFECT. After a dry run with the band clamps set to the right length, apply glue to each mitered surface and assemble the box.

USING BAND CLAMPS. Once you have verified that the joints are tight, crank down on the band clamps, but not so much that the webbing crushes the corners.

or easy and precise key slots cut on the tablesaw, use this cradle jig that carries the box at a 45° angle.

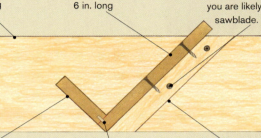

Plywood sleds, ¾ in. thick x 4 in. wide x 11 in. long

Rear support, ¾ in. thick x 6 in. wide x 6 in. long

Make sure all screws are above the highest level that you are likely to raise the sawblade.

Front support, ¾ in. thick x 2 in. wide x 6 in. long

Box supports are glued and biscuited together.

Support blocks, ¾ in. thick x 1 in. wide x 6½ in. long

CUTTING KEYS. The carriage jig registers against the fence of the tablesaw and slides on two sleds.

PREPARATIONS MAKE PERFECT. After a dry run with the band clamps set to the right length, apply glue to each mitered surface and assemble the box.

USING BAND CLAMPS. Once you have verified that the joints are tight, crank down on the band clamps, but not so much that the webbing crushes the corners.

support the piece as you pass it vertically by the sawblade. Then cut off a length of spline material.

You'll be working with some wide short-grain stock that will likely break in your capable hands, but that won't matter as long as the spline pieces fit snugly in the groove when you glue up. Make sure to cut the splines exactly to length, or a hair under, so that the miters still fit together nicely. Use a block plane and a bench hook to trim the splines to length or thickness. Leave the splines a bit wider than necessary and clean them after you're finished gluing up.

Unlock Different Looks with Keyed Miters

Pieces of wood inserted diagonally into the outside corner of miter joints are known as keys. Added after the box has been assembled, keys can be made from wood that matches the carcase or from a contrasting wood.

Hand-cut keyed miters–Place the box in a vise and, using your best backsaw, cut across the joint, making sure your sawcut depth is consistent on both sides. Use ve–

neer stock for the key and fit this to your sawcuts. If the veneer is too thick, pound it with a metal hammer. Don't worry if it's a bit loose; when the key hits the glue in the joint, it will swell up, providing a nice long-grain to long-grain joint. If you use the same wood, the keys almost disappear into the joint and the surrounding wood.

Keyed miters on the tablesaw–There are two jigs you can use to hold the work when you cut keyed miters on the tablesaw. For smaller boxes, a keyed miter jig run against the tablesaw fence works fine. Screw a straight fence to a piece of medium-density fiberboard (MDF) or plywood at a 45° angle. Make sure the screws are higher than any possible cut you'll ever make.

A more secure method for holding larger boxes is to use a cradle jig. Make this out of plywood or MDF with a right-angle support in the center. Hold the box in the cradle and run the jig right against the fence to make the cut.

After the first cut has been made, rotate the box for the next corner. When all four corners on the bottom are done, spin the box and do the matching joints for the top of the box. Use a flat-tooth blade for the nicest look, or clean up the bottom of the cuts with a ⅛-in. chisel.

On the bandsaw, rough out stock for the keys, making them oversize in width but close in thickness and long enough to hang on to. Your key stock should be inserted with its grain running parallel to the long grain of the box. Pass it by the tablesaw blade to trim it to size, using a thin push stick to hold it securely. When gluing in keys, use a hammer to tap down each key to the bottom of the slot on both sides of the corner.

Dovetails meet miters–Dovetailed keys employ the same keyed miter jig used on the tablesaw. A cradle jig also may be used, but you likely will need a dovetail bit with an extralong shaft for this jig. First, rough

Dovetailed Keys

KEYED MITER JIG

Auxiliary fence, ¾ in. thick x 5 in. wide x 12 in. long

Attach screws above the highest point of the bit.

Angle guide, ¾ in. thick x 2 in. wide x 10 in. long

TWO-STEP DOVETAILS. Remove part of the waste with a straight bit, then use a dovetail bit to cut the finished profile.

USE A DOVETAIL BIT TO FORM THE DOVETAIL KEY. Cut the stock higher than needed to provide a surface to ride against the fence.

THE RIGHT KEY. Check the fit of the key. If it is too tight, plane off a little from the bottom of the key.

Take the Top Off Your Box

Like the base, the lid fits into a groove in the box sides. After the box has been glued together, plan the spacing of the keys to match where the lid will be sawn off then saw it off with a tablesaw and a handsaw. Clean up the edges with a block plane and attach hinges.

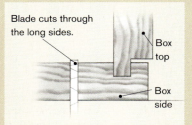

Blade cuts through the long sides.

Box top

Box side

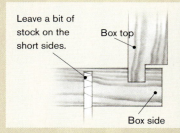

Leave a bit of stock on the short sides.

Box top

Box side

THROUGH-CUT. Set the tablesaw blade slightly higher than the thickness of the sides to cut through the two long sides.

PARTIAL CUT. Lower the blade to leave ¹⁄₁₆ in. of wood on the short sides. This alleviates clamping or supporting the lid with shims during the final cut.

FINAL CUT. Use a handsaw to cut through the two short sides. Clean up the edges of the box and the lid with a block plane.

out the waste with a straight bit, then set the dovetail bit to the final depth of cut and make the pass.

Mill the key stock out of a contrasting wood almost to width and taller than required. This way, when routing the keys, there will be some wood left to run against the fence. Use the same bit to rout the dovetail slots, but set it for a slightly taller cut to make the key stock, which will allow the keys to slide more easily into the slots. Trim both faces of the stock. If a key is just a hair too thick, plane off a shaving from the bottom where it's widest. Cut the keys overlong and glue them in place on the box. Clean up all your keyed miter joints on the bandsaw first. Then, working down and away from the corner of the box, use a block plane to smooth the keys. If you work toward the corner, you will tear out the short grain of the keys.

GARY ROGOWSKI runs the Northwest Woodworking Studio in Portland, Ore., and is a contributing editor to *Fine Woodworking* magazine.

Hand-Cut Keys

HAND-CUT KEY SLOTS.
Use a backsaw to cut diagonally into the corner. Make sure the depth of cut is even on both sides.

TENDERIZED VENEER. If the veneer spline is too thick to slide into the sawkerf, a few hammer blows will persuade it to fit.

THIN BUT STRONG. Despite its flexibility, the long-grain to long-grain glue bond strengthens the whole joint.

An Elegant Jewelry Box

BY STROTHER PURDY

Hand-cut mitered dovetails make the best of a subtle design.

Simple, rectangular jewelry boxes are easy to make. What's difficult is making them look nice. Without the benefit of curves, complex patterns, or inlays to give a box definition, the wood, joinery, and proportions become the all-important elements of the design. This box is made of curly Swiss pear, lined with apple on the inside and fitted with a walnut pull. The luscious grain and color of Swiss pear don't need additional embellishment to look stunning. I chose the apple and walnut primarily because they look good with the pear.

For the joinery, hand-cut dovetails with skinny little pins are classic, but they look like butt joints from the top and bottom edges. For a drawer, this detail doesn't matter. But on a jewelry box, framing the lid that way does not look attractive to my eye. To solve this problem, I mitered the dovetails on the lid and the bottom of the box (for more on the technique, see pp. 20–21). Mitered dovetails add interest and formality to the box without drawing undue attention to themselves.

As for the design and overall proportions, this jewelry box has shallow trays, so it should be relatively flat compared to its width and length. For the proportions, I used dimensions based on the golden rectangle, with a width-to-length ratio of about 1:1.6.

Mill the Lumber for the Best Match

A box is a great project to eat up some of the scrapwood lying around the shop. But there's nothing like making a box from a single, thick board. The color and grain will be very consistent, and by means of resawing, you can book-match panels. For this box, you'll need a board about 2 in. thick by 9 in. wide by 4 ft. long.

First, chalk out the parts, looking for the best grain patterns for the top and the least exciting for the trays. It's possible to resaw a 2-in.-thick board twice, making slices ⁷⁄₁₆ in. thick, and get three identical pieces with two options for book-matching.

Lay the boards on edge for a few days, with air circulating between them. This will help release any residual stresses in the wood. After that, mill the sides and top to dimension and glue up the top panel.

Finish the Top and Bottom Panels Before Assembly

For the top of the box, book-match the nicest pieces of wood and raise the panel. A raised-panel top softens the look of the box. For the bottom, use whatever wood is left over and leave it flat.

After cutting the dovetails and dry-fitting the sides of the box, take the dimensions for the top and bottom panels from the inside measurements, figuring in the added depth of the grooves. You can make the panels fit just so along their length, but across the width you need to account for changes in the relative humidity and subsequent shrinking or swelling that will occur. Rabbet the edges of the raised field, making

Make a Box from a Board

ONE BOARD, ONE BOX. A single source for the outside parts of this project ensures a more even grain and color match to the finished box.

RESAWING OFFERS TWO BENEFITS. By cutting thinner pieces of the same board, you can get book-matched panels and waste less lumber.

ASSEMBLE THE BOX, THEN SAW IT APART

The box and lid are constructed as a single unit and then cut apart after glue-up. This method guarantees a perfect fit between the box and lid.

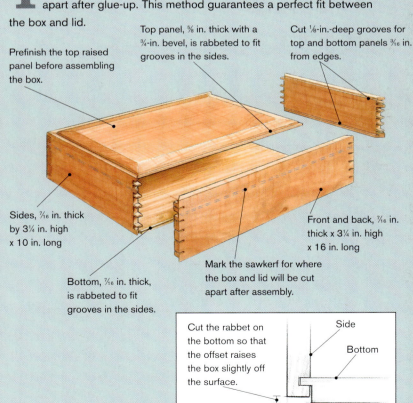

Prefinish the top raised panel before assembling the box.

Top panel, ⅝ in. thick with a ¾-in. bevel, is rabbeted to fit grooves in the sides.

Cut ⅛-in.-deep grooves for top and bottom panels ³⁄₁₆ in. from edges.

Sides, ⁷⁄₁₆ in. thick by 3¼ in. high x 10 in. long

Front and back, ⁷⁄₁₆ in. thick x 3¼ in. high x 16 in. long

Bottom, ⁷⁄₁₆ in. thick, is rabbeted to fit grooves in the sides.

Mark the sawkerf for where the box and lid will be cut apart after assembly.

Cut the rabbet on the bottom so that the offset raises the box slightly off the surface.

Side

Bottom

Mitered Dovetails Refine the Look of a Box

Dovetails with mitered edges are cut much like garden-variety dovetails, but they require a few extra steps. You have to be more careful marking the pieces, and they take a little longer to lay out and assemble.

1. Lay out the tails

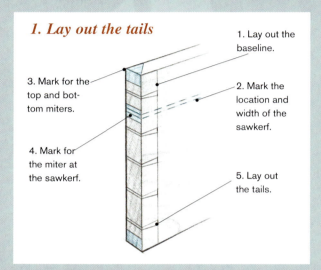

3. Mark for the top and bottom miters.

4. Mark for the miter at the sawkerf.

1. Lay out the baseline.

2. Mark the location and width of the sawkerf.

5. Lay out the tails.

2. Cut the tails and miters

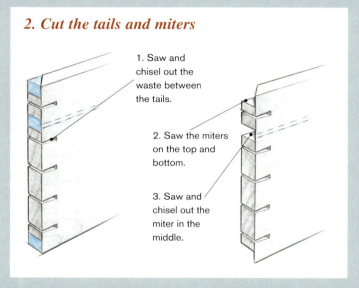

1. Saw and chisel out the waste between the tails.

2. Saw the miters on the top and bottom.

3. Saw and chisel out the miter in the middle.

Use a marking gauge to lay out the baselines on the faces of the boards. Lay out the sawkerf that will separate the lid from the box. Mark for the miters about ⅜ in. from the top and bottom edges. These lines represent the height of the miters. Now, scribe a line ⅛ in. above and below the sawkerf. Continue these lines from the baseline and around the edges on the inside faces of the pieces only. Finally, scribe the 45° angle on the top and bottom edges.

The mitered ends take the place of the traditional half-pins. There isn't room for a complete tail above the sawkerf, so you need to cut two half-tails. Below the sawkerf, divide the space equally to get three whole tails between four pins. I like to place the tails very close together, leaving only the width of a backsaw blade between them.

To clear out the waste between the tails, use a fine-toothed backsaw because you need to leave a very smooth surface on the inside. You can't go back later and clean it up with a chisel—there simply isn't room. After you cut one side, start the saw in the same kerf, angled the opposite way, to cut the second side.

To cut the miters on the edges, saw slightly off the line both from the edge and from the inside face. Cutting out the miters in the middle (where the lid and bottom will be cut apart) is a little harder. You can only cut them on an angle from the back, so you have to chisel out the waste. Pare the faces of the miters flat and smooth. You can make a jig to guide the angle of your cut if you prefer, but I find it's easier to do freehand.

them slightly too thick to fit the grooves, then fine-tune the fit with a shoulder plane, scraper, or sandpaper. Chamfer the top edges with a block plane—if you want machinelike precision, use a tablesaw or router.

Sand and prefinish the panels before assembling the box. A prefinished panel won't show an unfinished edge when it shrinks out of its groove. Also, lightly sand and prefinish the inside of the sides (I give them a few coats of shellac). The apple lining will cover most of the inside of the box, but not all of it.

CUT THE TAILS. A fine-toothed backsaw makes a clean and narrow kerf, and it offers good control over the cut.

CHOP OUT THE WASTE. The tight spaces left for very small pins require a ⅛-in. chisel to clean them out.

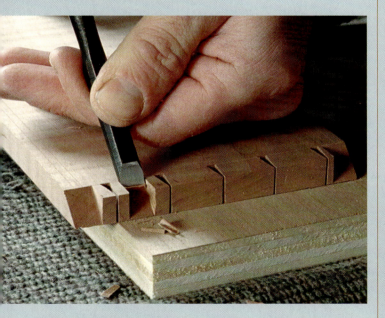

ROUGH-CUT THE OUTSIDE MITERS WITH A SAW. Then pare them to your pencil line with a chisel.

3. Cut the pins and the grooves for the panels

Just as you would for a regular set of dovetails, transfer the locations of the tails to the pin boards. At the same time, transfer the locations of the miters and cut them as you did on the tail boards.

Now is also a good time to cut the grooves for the panels. Put a rip blade in the tablesaw that cuts a flat-bottomed kerf. Set the blade to the desired depth and groove the panels along the inside top and bottom edges.

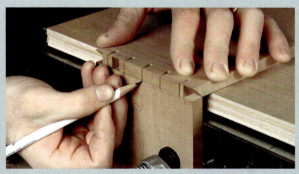

MARK THE PIN BOARDS FROM THE TAIL BOARDS. A clamp is worth as much as a steady hand when transferring the locations of pins.

MAKE ALL NECESSARY SAW CUTS IN THE PIN BOARDS. Chop out the waste between the pins (left). Pare the miters with a chisel (above).

Glue up the box (I use yellow glue), clamping evenly across the faces of the joint. Even pressure is important to avoid putting tension in the box. Later, when you saw apart an unevenly clamped box, the top and bottom could twist in different directions, making a bad fit. If the pins protrude from the tails, you'll need to make clamping cauls with fingers that put pressure only on the tails.

Let the glue cure thoroughly, then sand the exterior of the box to about 320 grit. Separate the lid from the bottom on the tablesaw, sawing the box in two parts along

CLEAN LINES AND SIMPLE DETAILS

Stunning wood, accomplished joinery, and pleasing proportions give this box a visual appeal. The shallow dimensions and removable trays on top make it easy to access the contents.

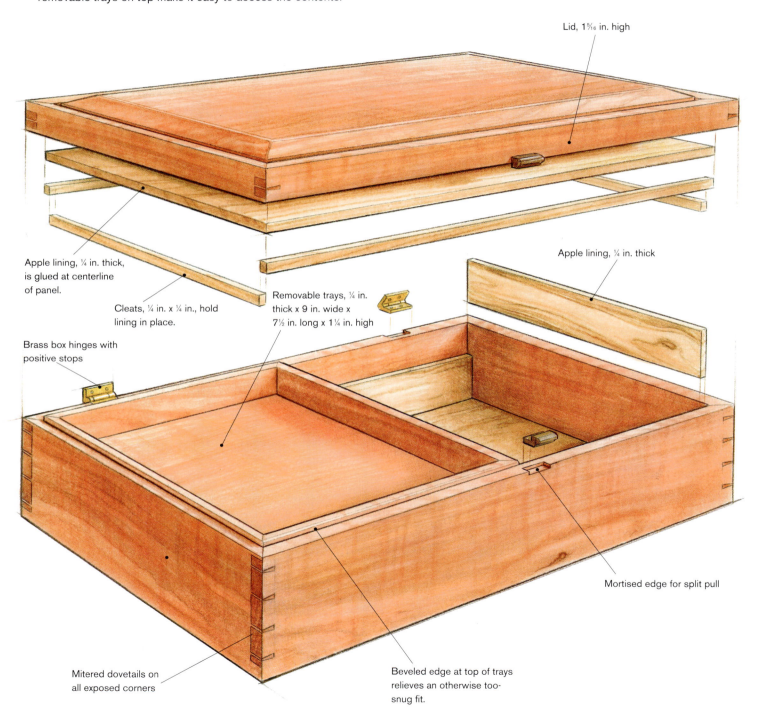

Lid, 1⁵⁄₁₆ in. high

Apple lining, ¼ in. thick, is glued at centerline of panel.

Cleats, ¼ in. x ¼ in., hold lining in place.

Removable trays, ¼ in. thick x 9 in. wide x 7½ in. long x 1¼ in. high

Apple lining, ¼ in. thick

Brass box hinges with positive stops

Mortised edge for split pull

Mitered dovetails on all exposed corners

Beveled edge at top of trays relieves an otherwise too-snug fit.

Saw Apart the Box and Install the Lining

A TABLESAWN JOINT NEEDS A LITTLE HELP. After setting the fence to the layout lines marked on the box, add masking tape around the outside of the box to minimize tearout during the cut. Clean up the sawn edges with a block plane, scraper, or sandpaper.

LEAVE A LITTLE BREATHING ROOM FOR THE LINING. After scraping off the shellac from the center of the underside of the lid, the author adds a bead of glue to secure the lining.

TRIM TO FIT. The side pieces are cut to fit and secured with a spot of glue.

the layout lines. Clean up the inside edges with a block plane, scraper, or sandpaper until the lid and bottom fit together seamlessly. The edges don't have to be perfectly square—I find they're easier to fit if they're angled in slightly. Sand the box to 400 grit, and finish it as you did the top panel.

Fit Hinges to the Box and Lid

Small box hinges (Brusso brand) are perfect for a project like this. The hinges are well made, and they have a positive stop when opened a little more than 90°—so you don't have to add a chain to keep the top from flapping open too far.

Use a marking gauge and a knife to lay out the position of the hinges. With a sharp chisel, chop out the waste, paring as necessary until each hinge leaf fits tightly. Now attach the hinges with two #3 steel screws. Instead of drilling for the screws—because they're so small—I made a pilot hole by tapping a small brad into the wood. When fitting the hinges, don't use the brass screws that come with them, because the brass is so soft that the screws will either break or their slots will get mangled. Put the brass screws in once and only once, after everything is done.

Line the Inside and Add the Trays

The apple wood I used to line this box came from a dead tree in my backyard.

Without such a source, I would have used another light-colored wood, such as cherry or maple. The lining should be thin enough to take up little interior space but not so thin that it warps—about ¼ in. thick is a good compromise.

Mill all of the lining pieces you'll need. Glue up panels for the inside of the lid and the bottom of the box if you don't have pieces wide enough. Sand them and apply several coats of shellac. These pieces need to be finished so that the bare wood does not come in contact with the contents of the box. Because wood is acidic, it will tarnish jewelry and ruin any valuable papers.

Fit the linings for the lid and box first, with a spot of glue in the center. Cut them so that they fit tightly along their lengths, but be sure to leave a little space on their sides to allow for wood movement. Cut the side pieces for the lid and box slightly long and press-fit them in place. Fit the long sides first, then the short sides. If the wood

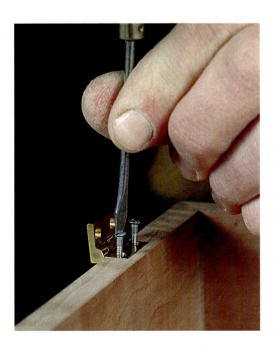

INSTALLING HINGES. Brass screws wear out easily, so it's best to use steel screws to temporarily fasten the hinges. Steel heads are less prone to stripping. Use the brass screws only for the final fit.

is especially flexible, spot-glue the liner parts in place.

The trays are simply smaller boxes made from the pear wood. Don't bother with fancy joinery for them—miters on single dovetails at the corners are fine. You can cut grooves for the bottoms, if you wish, but because these trays will never take much weight, simply gluing on the bottoms works quite well.

The height of the trays is critical. They sit proud of the seam between the box and the lid and form an airtight seal, keeping dust out of the box. Chamfer the top edges of the trays so that they are not abraded every time the lid is closed. To test-fit them, put the trays in place and open the lid. If the trays rise with the lid, they're too tight. Plane or sand the top edges until the trays stay in place when the lid is opened.

A Pull with a Twist

The small split pull I designed for this box doesn't call attention to itself, but it adds interest to an otherwise plain-looking front. When closed, the pull looks like one piece, but it's actually two pieces—one attached to the top edge of the box, the other to the underside of the lid. To open the lid, you need to twist your fingers one way. Trying it the other way makes it seem as if the lid is locked.

Make a slightly oversized rectangular piece of walnut for the pull and saw it in half. Mortise the two pieces so that they come together just so when closed, then glue them into place, unfinished. Cut and sand them to shape after they're installed.

Finish the outside of the box with a Danish oil mixture, shellac, varnish, or lacquer. Let the finish cure for a few days, then give the surface a good coat of wax and buff it to a high shine. Put the hinges back in, and your box is done.

STROTHER PURDY is a woodworker in Bridgewater, Conn., and a former associate editor of *Fine Woodworking* magazine.

Shaker Oval Boxes

BY JOHN WILSON

Oval boxes continue to be the most popular product the Shakers ever offered to the outside world. Originally produced for their practicality (nesting boxes inside each other required little storage space) and utility (almost anything and everything was stored in these durable containers), they have become collector's items for their simple beauty.

As testament to the boxes' enduring appeal, I've been able to make a living for the last 10 years by traveling around the country teaching Shaker box making to groups of woodworkers. Box making's appeal is that, in short order, you can have a stack of boxes, as shown in the photo at right, that any woodworker would be proud to show off or to give as gifts. In just a day and a half, my students, who range in ability from novice to advanced woodworkers, complete a stack of five traditional Shaker oval boxes.

The secret to the classes' efficiency is that we start with the tops, bottoms, and band material thicknessed and rough dimensioned. I also bring the necessary patterns and forms for cutting the band's fingers, bending and drying the bands, and shaping the tops and bottoms. I can supply all the

A STACK OF FIVE SHAKER BOXES can be built in just a couple of days, even by novice woodworkers, as the author proves in his classes many times every year. The boxes are great for display or storage and make gifts that everyone loves to receive.

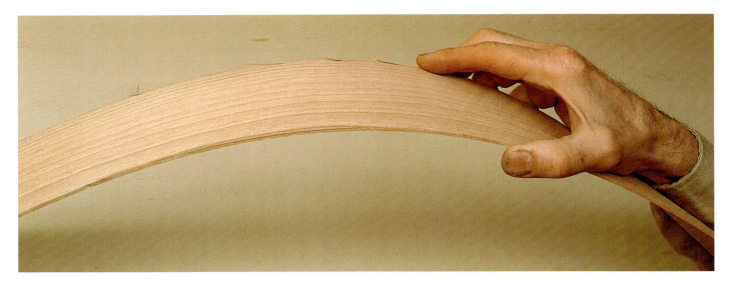

necessary materials, hardware, and forms if you want to make the boxes that way. But this article will show you how to prepare the stock and make your own patterns and forms.

There is no one right way to make an oval box, just as there is no one material for bands, no one system for numbering sizes of nesting boxes, nor one shape to the fingers. What can be said for the following procedure is that it works for me and for participants in my workshops to produce a stack of five boxes, from a small #0 to a #4 box, in the Shaker tradition. Because the #2 box is the mid-sized and easiest to work of the stack of five boxes, I suggest students start with it.

Selecting and Preparing Stock

Box bands for the base and the lid of an oval box are thin slices of hardwood, or thick veneers, that will bend and tack without splitting. The Shakers used maple, bands and pine tops and bottoms more than anything else. But there are a wide range of hardwoods that are suitable for box making including ash, cherry, walnut, apple, hackberry, hard and soft maple, and birch. Straight-grained wood is best for bending. Any wood can be used for the tops and bottoms.

I prefer quartersawn wood for both the bands and the tops and bottoms. In bands, the quartersawn grain reduces curling along the edges of the fingertips. Quartersawn wood is preferable for tops and bottoms because it has half the wood movement of flatsawn stock and is less likely to cause structural problems, especially in the larger sizes.

Moisture content also influences the workability and stability of the wood. Tops and bottoms should be dried to a moisture content (MC) of 8 percent to 9 percent to help prevent gaps showing up at the edges from shrinkage or splitting the band at the ends from expansion. Bands are easiest to work when air dried to 15 percent to 20 percent MC. Kiln drying band stock makes it brittle and more difficult to bend.

The thickness of the bands, tops, and bottoms varies with each size box, as shown in the chart on p. 29. The most difficult part of preparing box stock is thicknessing band stock. Smaller boxes require thinner bands to make the tighter radius bends, but the larger boxes need the heft of the thicker veneers.

When I first started making boxes, I resawed stock on my tablesaw. A sharp, carbide-tipped, 40-tooth blade yields a clean cut, and the 3-in. capacity of a 10-in. tablesaw is enough to cut bands for a #4 box in one pass. Tops and bottoms for up to a #4 box can be resawn by making a pass along each edge of the stock.

Most of the stock less than .10-in. thick that I use now is veneer-sliced to my specifications. These veneers are uniformly thick, and the knife leaves a smooth surface. But because the knife bends the wood during the cutting process, it can create checking in one side of the veneer. The checked side of the veneer will be more likely to split if placed on the outside of the box. The best way to determine the knife-checked face of veneer-sliced stock is to flex the band across its length in both directions. The side of the band that shows splitting or checking, as shown in the photo on the facing page, should be used as the box's inside surface. Then bending will help control the splitting.

If a band does split while bending, you can still salvage the stock. Trim off the split edges and make a shallower box, often called a button box, or add a handle and make a carrier. The Shakers also had plenty of odd-sized boxes and carriers, although such boxes are less common.

Patterns, Forms, and Hot-water Trays

I developed finger patterns and top and bottom oval patterns from drawings in *Measured Drawings of Shaker Furniture and Woodenware* by Ejner Handberg (Berkshire Traveller Press, Stockbridge, Mass., 1991). I then made permanent patterns from pre-painted aluminum coil stock used as trim by residential siding contractors for windows and doors. The coil stock cuts easily with a utility knife. Straight cuts are made by scoring the aluminum and then flexing it along the score. Curved lines can be scored freehand or cut with shears. I drilled

BEVELING THE FINGER EDGES AND ENDS is much easier if the band is first soaked in hot water and securely clamped to the bench. Reposition the hardboard cutting block for each finger set so that knife kerfs from previous cuts don't affect the cut.

TACKING BANDS WITH AN ANVIL BACKUP clinches the tack. Once tacked, the top band will be dried in place on the box band. Shapers in the box band on the bench keep the band's oval shape while it dries.

beveled edge stretches the oval band as the shaper is pushed deeper into the band. Two holes drilled through the shapers provide ventilation and a grip for pulling them out of the bands.

Another necessity for bending is a means of soaking the bands in hot water. I use a copper tray with a hinged lid, but a painted-steel window planter tray with a board on top also works well. Alternately, a vegetable drawer from an old refrigerator or a length of steel gutter with end caps and a plywood cover will do as well. An electric hot plate, as shown in the background of the photo at left, works great for heating the water.

Shaping the Fingers

Begin preparing the band stock by marking the finger pattern and tack locations, as shown in the drawing on p. 29, on the outside face of the band. Bandsaw the fingers along the layout lines to rough shape, and drill the ⁵⁄₆₄-in.-dia. tack pilot holes. Trim the fingers to finished form by clamping the band onto a Masonite cutting board and beveling the curved edge and end of each finger with a utility knife, as shown in the photo on p. 27. I find it much easier to make and control the cut if I soak the fingers in a glass of hot water for a few minutes first. Try to maintain the bandsawn shape, and keep the tip of the finger about ³⁄₁₆ in. wide. Note that the bevel is greatest at the bases of the fingers, about 20°, and decreases to about 10° at the tips.

The final step in preparing the band stock for bending is to feather the end of the band opposite the fingers. Tapering the last 1 in. to 1½ in. of the band eliminates a bump inside the box where the band ends. I prefer to taper the band on a belt sander using a scrap of wood to apply even pressure to the band. If you don't have a belt sander, then you can handplane this taper.

⁵⁄₆₄-in.-dia. holes to show where the copper tacks go.

Oval bottom patterns are made to the dimensions shown in the chart on p. 29. The top oval patterns are about ⅛ in. larger.

If you enlarge the bottom pattern by 2 percent on a copying machine, you will have a close approximation.

I use two different types of forms when making Shaker boxes. One form is the core around which I bend the bands, and the other form is the shaper that I plug into both sides of the bands for drying. By making up several sets of the shapers, I can mass-produce boxes with just one set of cores.

I made the cores out of pine or basswood, bandsawing them to rough shape and then disc or belt sanding them to refine the shape. The shapers are made from ½-in.-thick pine for the #0 and #1 boxes and ⅝-in.-thick pine for the #2 through #4 boxes. Use the same oval patterns as for the cores, but cut slightly outside the line at a 10° bevel. The shaper slides easily into the band, but the increasing diameter of the

SHAKER OVAL BOXES

The dimensions of oval box components vary depending upon the boxes. The chart below provides dimensions for the five most popular sizes.

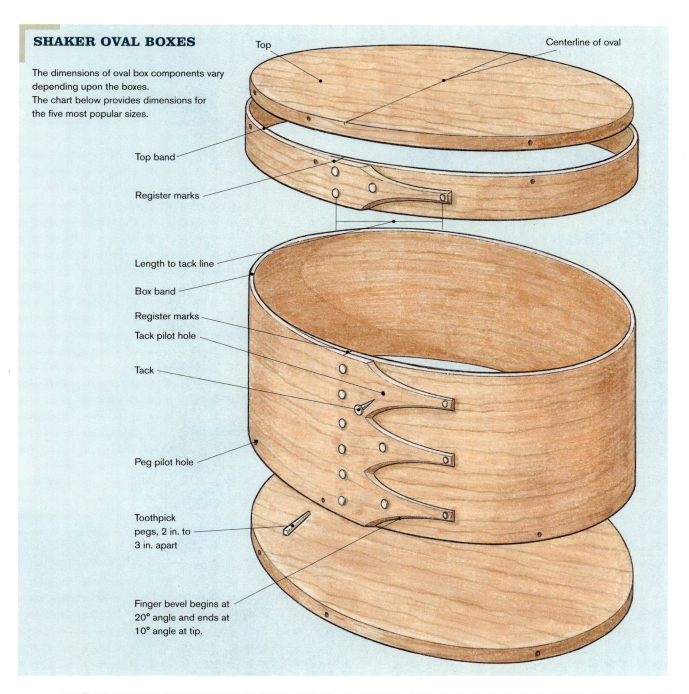

Top

Centerline of oval

Top band

Register marks

Length to tack line

Box band

Register marks

Tack pilot hole

Tack

Peg pilot hole

Toothpick pegs, 2 in. to 3 in. apart

Finger bevel begins at 20° angle and ends at 10° angle at tip.

OVAL BOX DIMENSIONS

Box size	Bottom oval* (WxL)	Top and bottom thickness	Box band (TxWxL)	Top band (WxL)	No. of fingers-length to tack line	Tack size
#0	1⅞ x 3½	.195	.060 x 1¹⁄₁₆ x 11⅞	⁷⁄₁₆ x 12¼	2 - 1⅝	1 or 1½
#1	2⁹⁄₁₆ x 4⁹⁄₁₆	.210	.062 x 1½ x 15	½ x 15½	2 - 1¾	1 or 1½
#2	3½ x 5¾	¼	.067 x 2 x 19	⅝ x 19¾	2 - 1⅞	1½
#3	4½ x 7	¼	.072 x 2½ x 23	1¹⁄₁₆ x 24	2 or 3 - 2¹⁄₁₆	1½
#4	5½ x 8¼	¼	.077 x 3¹⁄₁₆ x 27	¾ x 28	3 - 2¼	1

* Top oval about ⅛ in. larger than bottom oval.

Bending the Bands

Some folks shy away from projects that involve bending because they think it is difficult. However, the thin band stock, aided by a good soaking in hot water, bends easily around the core. You'll want to have everything ready, though, so you can bend the band before it cools, which it will do in about half a minute.

I soak the bands in hot water (180°F or hotter) for at least 10 minutes; 20 minutes will ensure that the troublesome bands are fully soaked (nothing is gained or lost after a half-hour). When ready, wrap the band around the core, making sure that the beveled side of the fingers faces out and that the tack line is aligned with the center of the oval core. If, during the bending process, you notice the veneer splitting or feathering, as shown in the photo on p. 26, stop. Turn the band inside out, rebevel the fingers, reheat the band, and rebend it with the better side out. From this point until the band is tacked together, be sure to hold all the fingers all the time or the band is likely to split up the middle between the fingers.

With the band wrapped around the core and the tack line centered on the core, draw a register mark across the top edges of the overlapped section at the front of the band. This register mark lets you open the band to release the core and then to push the band back together into the same size oval shaped on the core. Hammer the copper tacks and clinch them at the same time by nailing over a pipe anvil, as shown in the photo below, to secure the fingers.

The top band is made by repeating all the steps for the box band, except the box band is used instead of a core to bend the top band. After tacking the top band, slide it back on the box band to dry.

Let the bands air dry for two days before continuing. Oval shapers pushed into the top and bottom of the band will maintain their shape. You can speed up the process with a fan, but this can increase the edge curling around the fingers.

WHEN WRAPPING A BOX BAND AROUND THE CORE, be sure the beveled fingers face out and that the tack line is centered on the oval. An electric hot plate heats the copper tray in which the bands are soaked for about 20 minutes before bending.

Fitting Tops and Bottoms

Before proceeding with the top and bottom, I like to sand the inside of the box and top bands with 120-grit sandpaper. I also make sure the ends of the bands feather well into the inside contours while it's still easy to get at these surfaces.

To mark the oval shapes for the tops and bottoms, you can make appropriate-sized patterns for each box size or you can use the bands themselves as patterns. It usually doesn't make any difference when making the bottoms because the shapers have made the bands oval. But the top bands have a bump in them where they were wrapped over the fingers of the box band. On the #0 through #4 boxes, a pattern-shaped top can even out the oval. On larger boxes, the band is thicker and doesn't stretch so easily. Therefore, on the larger sizes, using the band for a pattern gives a better fit.

Once the bottom is marked and roughly bandsawn to shape, the final fitting is done on a disc sander with the table set to bevel the edge 4°. The cork effect of the beveled edge provides a tight fit between the bottom and the band where the edge has been flared by the shapers. Check the fit frequently as you gradually sand to the line. The bottom should be snug but not overly tight.

Finger direction on a box is determined by the side of the band on which the bottom is fitted. Most boxes have fingers pointing to the right, although left-pointing fingers are not uncommon. Top band fingers always point in the same direction as the bottom band. Determine which direction you want your fingers to point, and insert the bottom by fitting it against the front lap of the band and into both ends; then stretch the back of the band over the opposite edge. Press the bottom into place until the entire rim of the band is slightly above the surface.

When the bottom is pressed firmly into place, lightly sand it level on the belt sander. Now you also have a good opportunity to hide any gaps between the bottom and the band. First work some glue into the gap, and then immediately sand the bottom, either on the belt sander or by hand. The sanding dust will mix with the glue to form a filler that blends perfectly with the box.

The bottom is held in place with square, wooden pegs (toothpicks) driven into predrilled pilot holes. Pilot holes are $\frac{1}{16}$ in. dia. for the #0 and #1 boxes and $\frac{5}{64}$ in. dia. for #2 and larger boxes. Drill holes equally spaced around the box, 2 in. to 3 in. apart, tap the pegs into the holes, and snip off the ends with diagonal cutters. You can then sand the toothpicks flush or trim them with a utility knife.

The top is made following the same procedure as for the bottom. However, a loose-fitting top band can be snugged up by changing the shape of the top oval. Elongating the top oval will move the slack in the band to the ends of the oval, causing the band to hug the box in the middle for a positive friction fit.

Finish the Box

Shaker boxes can be painted, varnished, or oiled. Before the mid-1800s, the Shakers usually painted their boxes. In later years, they varnished them. I use a clear lacquer on my boxes after hand-sanding the outside with 120-grit paper. I first brush on a sanding sealer, followed by a coat of lacquer. Although many woodworkers like the ease of application of an oil finish, I don't like the odor that lingers for months inside the closed boxes. Lacquer and shellac also give the sharpest image to my favorite bird's-eye maple tops.

JOHN WILSON is a Shaker box maker, instructor and supplier of parts, hardware and related tools in Charlotte, Mich.

Sources

Contact the author directly for details on classes in your area or information on his complete line of Shaker box supplies and instructional material:

The Home Shop
500 E. Broadway Hwy.
Charlotte, MI 48813
517-543-5325

Building a Humidor

BY RICK ALLYN

You can smoke a dry cigar, but you won't enjoy it. It will burn too hot, making the smoke acrid and unpleasant. Most of the flavor and all the subtleties of the tobacco will be lost. Cigars are made in the tropics, where the relative humidity is a constant 70 percent, and they should be kept at that level. The

relative humidity in Southern Idaho, where I live, is about 30 percent in the summer, and lower in the winter—a really hostile environment for cigars. I have had cigars dry up, even unwrap, four hours after I bought them.

A properly functioning humidor is a necessity for enjoying good cigars anywhere outside of the tropics. With only monthly upkeep, a well-made humidor will preserve cigars indefinitely. Very fine cigars even improve when aged in a humidor.

Building a humidor that works is not as simple as making a nice box and fitting a humidification device in it. This is often how they're made, and the results are cigars ruined from too little or too much moisture. Maintaining 70 percent humidity is a balancing act that depends in large part on the wood you use and the tightness of the lid's seal. It's not rocket science, but making a good humidor takes some care in design and execution.

Why use Spanish Cedar?

The wood you choose to make and line the humidor is particularly important. It should not have an unpleasant smell or taste because the cigars will pick it up. The wood also should be porous so it will first absorb, then release moisture evenly, while remain-

NOT JUST PRETTY BOXES. Humidors need to be carefully constructed if they are to maintain the right humidity for cigars.

SIMPLE JOINERY MAKES A STURDY BOX

The front, back, and sides of the box are cut from one long piece of veneered Spanish cedar. The top is veneered MDF; the bottom is plywood. All the joints are rabbets and depend on precise fitting for strength.

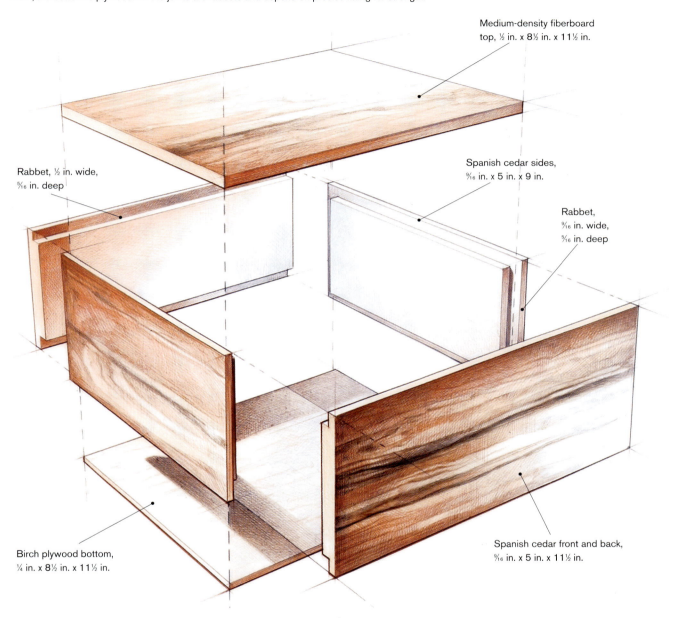

Medium-density fiberboard top, ½ in. x 8½ in. x 11½ in.

Rabbet, ½ in. wide, ⁵⁄₁₆ in. deep

Spanish cedar sides, ⁹⁄₁₆ in. x 5 in. x 9 in.

Rabbet, ⁹⁄₁₆ in. wide, ⁵⁄₁₆ in. deep

Birch plywood bottom, ¼ in. x 8½ in. x 11½ in.

Spanish cedar front and back, ⁹⁄₁₆ in. x 5 in. x 11½ in.

ing dimensionally stable. The wood will reach 70 percent moisture content on the inside, while the humidity on the outside could be as low as 20 percent. For many woods, this is a recipe for severe cupping.

Spanish cedar is the traditional and best choice for a humidor. When kiln dried, it is very stable and will not warp or grow much when it reaches 70 percent moisture content. Its oils inhibit the growth of

molds and mildew that destroy cigars. Spanish cedar has a delicate aroma that is complementary, enhancing the cigar's taste.

Spanish cedar does have one serious problem: bleeding sap. It will ooze out of the wood, stick to your cigars, and ruin them. Pieces that look sap-free can bleed many months after the humidor is finished. Common advice is that South American cedar (Cedrela fissilis) has a sap problem,

RABBET THE FOUR SIDES AT ONCE, while they're still one piece. A dado blade will make the cut in one pass.

CUT THE RABBETED SIDES APART and to length on the tablesaw. Use a stop block to ensure consistent lengths.

and the Central American varieties (Cedrela odorata and C. mexicana) do not. However, I have found little difference between them. There are ways to reduce the problem with sap. The thinner you slice the cedar, the less sap the piece will bleed later. Kiln drying, if well done, will set the sap. And if you do get some sap on the surface, acetone or lacquer thinner will take it off.

One-sided Veneering for the Basic Box

Because I build humidors professionally, I make a variety of designs. But they're all simple and easy to build. The only joints are rabbets and grooves. I use Spanish cedar for the sides and the top, veneering only the outside. I glue up the whole box at once, and put a solid-wood edge-band along every side. Then I cut the box into top and bottom halves on a bandsaw. One of my favorite styles uses pau ferro (Machaerium spp.) veneer with wenge edge-banding and holly and mahogany inlay (see the photo on the facing page).

The most common box size I make is 12 in. by 9 in. by 5 in. with internal dimensions of 10½ in. by 7½ in. by 3⅝ in. It will store about two boxes of cigars, 50 in all. Cigars range from 4½ in. to 8 in. long and 35 to 52 ring size (about ½ in. to just over ¾ in. dia.). Most commonly, however, they are about 6 in. long by 42 ring. If you buy a much longer cigar, it can go in sideways.

For the front, back, and two sides, I mill a single piece ⁵⁄₁₆ in. thick, 5 in. wide, and about 48 in. long. For the top, I use a piece of 8½-in. by 11½ in. medium-density fiberboard (MDF), ½ in. thick. The MDF adds weight to help keep the lid closed. I veneer all the Spanish cedar on one side, but for the bottom, I use ¼-in. birch plywood without any veneer.

Now, I know we all have been taught to veneer both sides of anything, but this is an exception. Perhaps it is a combination of

A TABLESAW MAKES THE EDGE-BANDING AND INLAY JOINTS A CINCH. Four cuts along each edge create the necessary joints.

Rabbets for Edge-Band and Inlay

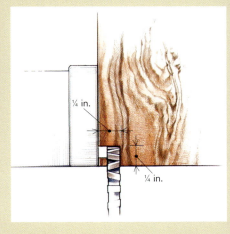

For the edge-banding, make ¼-in. x ¼-in. cuts along the top and sides. Make the bottom cuts ¼ in. x ⅛ in. deep.

¼ in.

¼ in.

For the inlay, make ⅛-in. x ¹⁄₁₆-in.-deep cuts along the edge-banding rabbets.

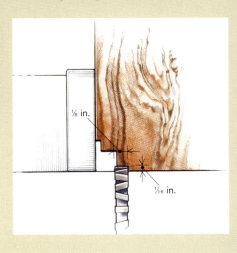

⅛ in.

¹⁄₁₆ in.

things that makes it work: the stability of the cedar, the stability of the box construction, the constant humidity on the inside, the lacquer finish on the outside. Anyway, it works. I have never had a box come apart using this technique.

With a dado head, I cut ½-in.-wide rabbets ⁵⁄₁₆ in. deep along both long edges of the piece of cedar. Next I cut it to the lengths necessary for the front, back, and side pieces. On the side pieces only, I cut ⁵⁄₁₆-in.-wide rabbets ⁵⁄₁₆ in. deep on the ends to form the corner joints (see the drawing on p. 33).

I dry-clamp the front, back, and sides together with several band clamps. Only at this point do I carefully trim the top and bottom to size in a crosscut box for an exact fit. The joints of the top and bottom provide a great deal of strength to the humidor and should be right on.

After the dry-fitting, I glue the box together. I use a reactive polyurethane glue from Custom-Pak Adhesives because it is waterproof, sets slowly enough to make clamping up a stress-free job, and has a

clamp time of just over an hour. Waterproof glue is a necessity on the corner joints because they will eventually live in a high-moisture environment. Even the waterproof type II polyvinyl acetate (PVA) glues will eventually let go if exposed to so much water for long. At the same time, I have used regular PVA glue for the veneering,

YELLOW GLUE AND TAPE ATTACH THE EDGE-BANDING. Wenge edge-banding is butted at the corners, not mitered, because end grain is not conspicuous.

with everyday handling. I add inlay along the edge-banding for contrast. The result is visually pleasing and reasonably durable.

After the box has been glued together, I cut rabbets along each edge of the box for the edge-banding (see the photos and drawings on p. 35). I make the rabbets ¼ in. by ¼ in. along the top and sides. And I make them ¼ in. by ⅛ in. deep on the bottom because the edge is thinner.

Along the cuts for the edge-banding, I make a second series of cuts for the inlay, ⅛ in. wide and ¹⁄₁₆ in. deep. The veneer on the edge of these cuts cannot have any breakout. I use an alternate-bevel, 80-tooth blade to cut the cross-grain rabbets and a 24-tooth flat-top blade to cut the long-grain rabbets.

Next I cut the pieces of ⁵⁄₁₆-in.-sq. wenge edge-banding to length, fit, and glue one piece at a time. Each piece simply butts against the other because the wenge end grain is difficult to discern from the long grain. First I apply the banding along the bottom edge, then around the top, and, finally, along the sides. I use yellow glue and 3M long masking tape to clamp each piece (see the top photo at left). This tape stretches for a stronger grip but won't pick up the grain when I pull it off.

When the edge-banding sets, I remove any squeeze-out from the inlay grooves with a small chisel. I cut the one-piece inlay to length and miter each corner. Then I run a bead of yellow glue down the groove and press in the inlay with the back of a chisel (see the bottom photos at left). Don't bother trying to clamp it in; the press-fit should hold it in place. When it dries, I plane the edge-banding level with the inlay and veneer, round the edges, and file down the end grain on the corners. Then I use a cabinet scraper to smooth the whole box.

PRESS THE INLAY INTO THE GROOVE WITH THE BACK OF A CHISEL (left). It should not need clamping or taping. Fine-tune the miter if necessary (above).

edge-banding, and inlay without a problem. Because the polyurethane glue is activated by moisture, I spray a little water on the joints before gluing up the box.

Edge-Banding to Resist Wear

Spanish cedar is a soft, lightweight wood, and the veneer isn't much more durable. I use a hard, solid wood edging for protection against the dings and dents that come

Bandsawing the Box Open and Fitting the Hardware

Building the box in one piece and then slicing it open is the best way to ensure a perfectly matching top and bottom. I perform this delicate operation on a bandsaw with a ½-in., 3-teeth-per-inch (tpi) blade with very little set. It makes this cut quickly and removes a minimum of wood.

I use a tall fence and set it so the top will be 1⅜ in. thick. Then I cover the cut line with masking tape to prevent breakout. With a careful push through the saw, it's done. I use a cabinet scraper to smooth the edges and make them perfectly flat. Ideally, the joint should be hard to distinguish when the box is closed. I use Brusso quadrant hinges, because they are well made, look nice, and are strong enough to keep the heavy lid from going anywhere. I install a box lock with a flush escutcheon on the outside.

The Lining Creates the Seal

For the lining, I use pieces of Spanish cedar ³⁄₁₆ in. thick. The cedar covers all six sides inside the box and is fitted to create a seal between the lid and the bottom of the box. I leave the lining unfinished to let it absorb and release moisture efficiently.

Before I fit the lining, I spray a coat of flat lacquer on the inside of the box except along the top and bottom edges. The lacquer slows down absorption of moisture into the joints when seasoning the humidor and slows down the release of moisture when the cigars are in it. The corner joints will appreciate the reduction in stress.

I install the top and bottom pieces of lining first. I cut them to fit snugly in length but leave a gap of ⅛ in. to ³⁄₁₆ in. on the sides for cross-grain movement. The lining for the sides in the bottom half of the box should extend above the edge by about ³⁄₁₆ in., and the lining in the top should be recessed by about ¼ in. (less if you desire a tighter seal). Next I install the lining along the sides of the top and the bottom: front and back pieces first, then the shorter sides. One thin bead of yellow glue down the middle of each piece will keep it centered during assembly.

The joint between the edge of the lid and the lining around the bottom will establish how well your humidor holds its humidity (see the drawing on p. 35). If the joint's too tight, not only will the box be difficult to open and close, it also will force the humidity level beyond 70 percent, making the air musty from poor circulation and increasing the chance of mold. A damp cigar will not burn well, and it will produce smoke too thick and pungent to be enjoyable. Like wood, a cigar that absorbs too much moisture may split. And if left soggy for too long, a cigar will begin to rot. But too loose a joint will let in drafts and make it difficult for the humidor to reach 70 percent relative humidity and remain there.

If you will be opening the humidor every few days, make the seal tight so that a dropped lid will float closed on a cushion of trapped air. If you won't be opening the humidor very often, make the seal less tight to help keep the air from becoming too damp.

Opening and closing should be easy, and you should just feel the lining touching on the lid as it shuts. For a tight seal, cut a steep bevel on the lining in the bottom of the box, and for a loose seal, make the bevel lower. The front needs more of a bevel than the sides and back so the lid opens and closes properly. I bevel all sides for even breathing and to maintain a continuity of style.

Sources

Beall Tool Co.
541 Swans Road NE
Newark, OH 43055
800-331-4718

Custom-Pak Adhesives
11047 Lamb's Lane
Newark, OH 43055
800-454-4583

Whitechapel Ltd.
P.O. Box 136
Wilson, WY 83014
800-468-5534

Woodcraft Supply
P.O. Box 1686
Parkersburg, WV 26102
800-225-1153

A BOX INSIDE OF A BOX

The Spanish cedar lining inside the humidor is in effect a second box. It maintains the humidity level by absorbing and releasing moisture from the humidifier. When the humidor's closed, the lining forms an almost-airtight seal around the edge.

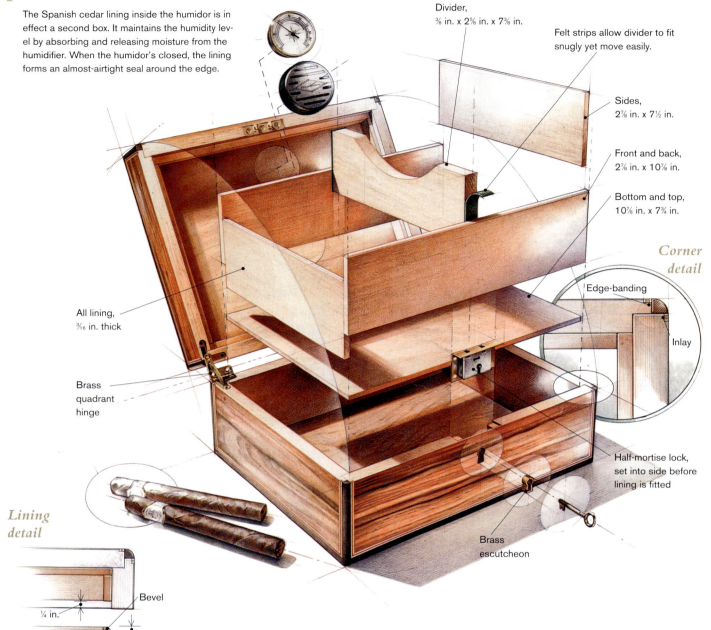

Divider,
⅜ in. x 2⅝ in. x 7⅝ in.

Felt strips allow divider to fit snugly yet move easily.

Sides,
2⅞ in. x 7½ in.

Front and back,
2⅞ in. x 10⅞ in.

Bottom and top,
10⅞ in. x 7¾ in.

Corner detail

Edge-banding

Inlay

All lining,
³⁄₁₆ in. thick

Brass quadrant hinge

Half-mortise lock, set into side before lining is fitted

Brass escutcheon

Lining detail

Bevel

¼ in.

³⁄₁₆ in.

Box side

Inner lining

Finishing the Humidor and Installing a Humidifier

I finish the outside with several coats of lacquer. I apply two or three coats of sanding sealer and then about 10 coats of gloss lacquer, sanding after every three coats. After the last coat, I let the finish cure for at least a week and then sand with 1,000-grit and water and power buff with automotive glazing compounds. Let the finish cure for as long as you can before waxing.

The humidifier provides a source of moisture in the box. Most humidifiers are extremely simple. A spongelike material, often florist's foam, is contained in a plastic or metal vented case. Because moisture from the humidifier falls, I attach the humidifier to the center of the lid for the most even distribution.

To help the humidifier stay put, I seal the cedar right behind it with lacquer. Even with the humidifier at the top of the

SAW THE TOP OFF THE BOX ON A BANDSAW. Tape the entire saw line and use a ½-in., 3-tpi blade to avoid breakout.

GENTLY PRESS-FIT THE LINING AROUND THE INTERIOR. When you season the humidor, the lining will swell and lock itself in place.

CAREFUL WITH THAT BEVEL ANGLE. It determines the rate the humidor loses humidity and receives fresh air. A humidor that is opened frequently should have a tighter fitting lid.

box, the bottom will be more humid. If you leave cigars in your humidor for a long time, rotate their position once a month.

The humidifier I prefer to use is the Nonpareil. It is made of anodized aluminum and uses a removable and easy-to-clean urethane foam pad. This eliminates the need to mess with distilled water because mineral deposits that would otherwise clog the humidifier can be washed out. Many humidifiers do not come apart for cleaning.

Before you put any cigars in your humidor, it's essential to season it first. After I fill the humidifier, I put a cup filled with wet paper towels in the closed humidor. It will take a few days for the box to reach 70 percent moisture content.

To monitor the humidity level of your humidor, you can attach a hygrometer to the bottom of the lid in the same way that you did with the humidifier. Remember that dial hygrometers are rarely accurate. The feel of the cigar is always the best measure of a properly functioning humidor. A good cigar should feel soft but not spongy or crunchy.

RICK ALLYN used to make guitars, but now designs and builds studio furniture and humidors. He attended the College of the Redwoods. He lives in Twin Falls, Idaho.

Thomas Jefferson's Writing Desk

BY LON SCHLEINING

In the spring of 1776, 33-year-old Thomas Jefferson had an idea. His frequent 200-mile coach rides from his home near Charlottesville, Va., to the Continental Congress in Philadelphia, Pa., could be more productive, he thought, if he could do some reading and writing on the way. After sketching his idea for a portable lap desk that would hold his supplies, he gave the drawing to Benjamin Randolph, a Philadelphia cabinetmaker. In July 1776, when the desk was brand new, Jefferson used it to write the Declaration of Independence.

This tiny writing desk, weighing only 5 lbs., is the result of Jefferson's ability to invent the obvious: a portable desk where he could keep all of his reading supplies and write comfortably. Jefferson used the desk for 50 years. The desk accompanied him wherever he went. In 1825, just a few months before his death, Jefferson gave the desk to his grandson, Joseph Coolidge. Soon after Coolidge's death in 1880, his children gave the desk to the federal government for safekeeping.

The moment I saw Jefferson's little lap desk in the Smithsonian National Museum of American History, I knew I had to build one. On numerous visits to Washington, D.C., I peered endlessly at the original, taking several rolls of photos and filling a notebook with sketches. Crafted out of mahogany, the desk has exquisitely small dovetails in the drawer, tiny screws fastening the hinges, and a small satinwood inlay for decoration. When opened, the desk offers a comfortably slanted, baize-covered writing surface. (Baize is a feltlike fabric used to cover billiard tables.) The lid's support stand fits into different notches so that Jefferson could change the angle of the top when he

REVOLUTIONARY LAPTOP.
Thomas Jefferson wrote much of the Declaration of Independence on this small mahogany desk. The original (at right) is in the Smithsonian Institution.

wished. Folded halfway, it becomes a book rest. A mortise in the underside of the lid houses the arms and allows the lid to close completely. The single drawer has compartments for an inkwell, writing quills, nibs, pen knife, and paper.

I finally found rough dimensions for the piece in an out-of-print book about the desk, *Declaration of Independence Desk: Relic of Revolution* by Silvio Bedini (Smithsonian Institution Press). Using rough dimensions and photos I found in the book, I was able to reproduce the drawings for the desk, then build a replica of the desk itself. Though it looks very simple, the desk turned out to be one of the most interesting and challenging woodworking projects I've built. It is deceptively intricate with lots of tiny parts—just my kind of project.

Drawings Reproduced from Photos

The first task in building the desk was to reproduce the working drawings. I began by drawing the perimeter of the piece full size. Then, using photos—both my own and from the book—I slowly filled in the details.

I made an enlarged copy of a photograph and then transferred the known dimensions —such as the width of the desk—to the copy. Using dividers and an inch scale, I was able to figure out other dimensions. Though the result is not 100 percent accurate, it's pretty close.

When scaling from photographs, you have to take distortion into account. The camera foreshortens the object, making it larger in the front and smaller as it becomes more distant, so a little bit of guesswork is involved. One other useful trick with photos is to photocopy them. Enlarging the photos a little at a time, I was able to get full-scale copies, which made measuring details like the dovetail spacing much easier.

Shopmade Plywood-Core Panels Provide Stability

The original desk is made of mahogany, except for a small satinwood inlay around the drawer front and a matching inlay on the back of the case. Most of the material is ⅜ in. thick, but the drawer parts are much more delicate, as thin as ⅛ in.

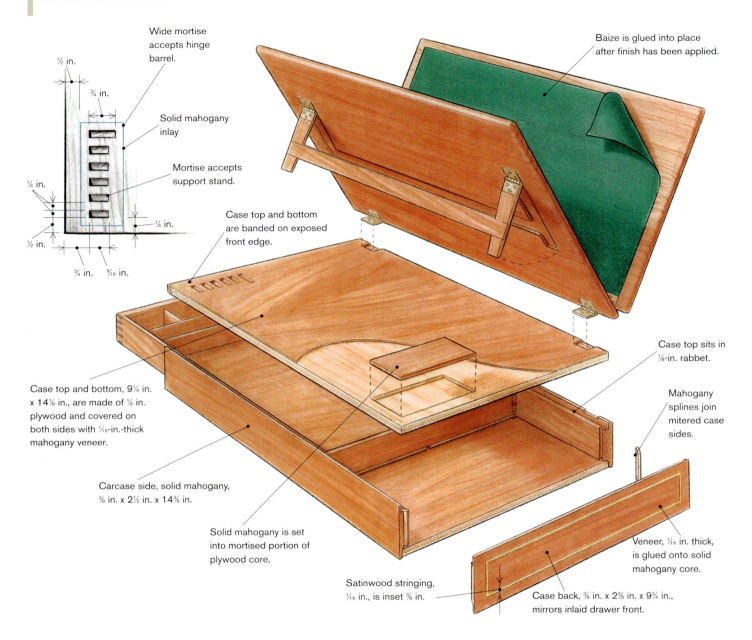

½ in.

¾ in.

Wide mortise accepts hinge barrel.

Solid mahogany inlay

Mortise accepts support stand.

¼ in.

¼ in.

½ in.

¾ in.   ⁹⁄₁₆ in.

Baize is glued into place after finish has been applied.

Case top and bottom are banded on exposed front edge.

Case top and bottom, 9¼ in. x 14⅛ in., are made of ¼ in. plywood and covered on both sides with ¹⁄₁₆-in.-thick mahogany veneer.

Carcase side, solid mahogany, ⅜ in. x 2½ in. x 14⅜ in.

Solid mahogany is set into mortised portion of plywood core.

Satinwood stringing, ¹⁄₁₆ in., is inset ⅜ in.

Case top sits in ⅛-in. rabbet.

Mahogany splines join mitered case sides.

Veneer, ¹⁄₁₆ in. thick, is glued onto solid mahogany core.

Case back, ⅜ in. x 2⅜ in. x 9¾ in., mirrors inlaid drawer front.

I could have slavishly duplicated the chest, imperfections and all, but I decided instead to incorporate modern materials, tools, and techniques—such as using plywood-core veneered panels.

Countless changes in humidity caused the original desk's solid flatsawn mahogany panels to cup so badly that the screws holding the hinges appear to have been torn loose and repaired numerous times. It would be much easier to make these panels out of solid wood, as Randolph did—and

it's an option you may want to consider—but I decided to deal with wood movement by making built-up panels consisting of a plywood core and bandsawn mahogany veneer. I figured the plywood core would stabilize the panels.

It's simple enough to buy sliced veneer, but I wanted more control over the thickness and grain pattern. To make your own veneer, you need a bandsaw and a benchtop surface planer. I cut the veneer a little thicker than ⅛ in. on a 14-in. bandsaw with a riser block, which allowed a full 10-in.-wide cut. If your bandsaw won't support a cut this wide, simply cut two 5-in. pieces and glue them together. When setting up the bandsaw, be sure to take drift angle into account.

Joint or plane one face of the mahogany, make the bandsaw cut, then surface the face of the board once more. The veneers will be smooth on one side but rough on the other. The veneer is too thin and flexible to run through the planer on its own, so tape the veneer—smooth side down—onto a piece of melamine, using double-faced tape. The whole assembly can be run through the planer, which will give you a clean surface on both sides.

Gluing the veneer to the core–The first job of gluing up the panels is to cap the plywood edges and inlay areas that will be mortised out for the desk support stand and the notches in the top of the carcase panel. I ran all of the grain in the same direction so that it would look like a single, solid piece of mahogany, end grain and all. First mill some mahogany to the thickness of the Baltic birch plywood core. For the long edges, rip strips about ¼ in. wide. Carefully cut some pieces of end-grain edging about ¼ in. wide. This edging—quite fragile when first cut—gets reinforced when the veneer is glued in place. By cutting the banding out of the same piece of wood you use for the veneer, the color and grain pattern should be pretty close.

Rout out the areas where the mortises will go and glue in mahogany pieces, carefully outlining the backing areas on the outside of the veneer so you'll know what goes where after the veneer has been glued on. Glue the mahogany into the mortise, then use a cabinet scraper to flush it to the plywood core.

The plywood is sandwiched between layers of veneer, and all of the panels are glued up at once. To save time, use a roller

Edge-Banding is the Key to Seamless Veneering

MAKING VENEER ON THE BANDSAW. Slicing veneer isn't hard as long as your bandsaw is tuned up and working well. A new blade, a riser block, an auxiliary fence set to the drift angle, and a nice, easy feed pressure will help you achieve a very satisfying cut.

CUTTING THE PLYWOOD BAND. For a seamless edge that will look like solid wood, cut banding from the end grain of the same mahogany board you used to cut the veneer.

GLUING THE BANDING IN PLACE. The perimeter of the plywood is banded with mahogany prior to gluing the veneer. The end grain is fragile at this point, but the glued-on veneer will provide reinforcement.

INLAY THE PLYWOOD CORE. Because the top of the carcase and the writing surfaces will be mortised to accommodate the support stand, the plywood is mortised and inlaid with solid wood. After using a Forstner bit to remove the bulk of the material, a straightedge jig helps guide a laminate trimmer to clean up the edges.

ROLL ON THE GLUE. Use a roller to apply glue to both the veneer and the plywood core, making sure that there is 100% coverage on both.

MORTISING FOR THE SUPPORT STAND. The lower writing surface of the desk is mortised to accept the support stand. After material has been hogged out with a router, a chisel is used to square up the corners.

to apply glue to both the plywood and the veneer. With one layer of melamine between the panels, stack more layers of melamine, sandwiching the panels to help distribute clamp pressure evenly. Once the glue has set, the veneer can be trimmed flush with the edges.

Straightforward Carcase Construction

The carcase for the original desk consists of five boards joined with rabbet joints and a few brads. The grain orientation of the top and bottom panels is across the width of the desk. The end is mitered and has satinwood stringing matching that of the drawer front on the opposite end of the desk. The miter joints in the original probably have hidden dovetails, but I used splined miter joints instead.

Again, I opted to glue up veneered panels for the top and bottom of the carcase, although in the original these solid mahogany panels are nailed to rabbets in the sides of the desk and seem to have stayed flat just fine. If you glue up plywood-core panels, you must inlay mahogany where the notches are in the top panel. Because only one edge on each of the panels shows, only that edge needs banding.

Inlay the satinwood detail—At about 1⁄16 in. wide, the stringing on the end piece looks like it was set into a slot in the original. But I approached it as a marquetry project. Using a razor knife and straightedge to cut the pieces, glue up the veneer with the stringing in place. Then glue the veneer back on to the substrate, in my case a piece of solid mahogany.

Rabbets and hidden splines hold the case together—The spline cuts are easily made using a tablesaw sled. Place the carcase parts flat on the sled and angle the blade at 45°. Use a stop block to register the cut, and make sure that the cut is

PLYWOOD CORE STABILIZES HINGED WRITING SURFACES

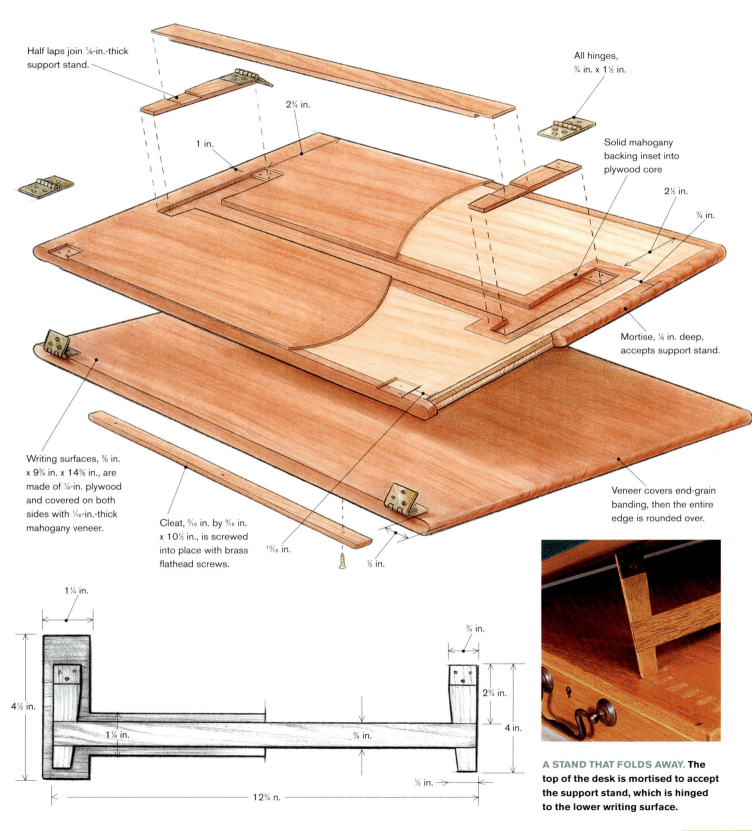

Half laps join ⅛-in.-thick support stand.

All hinges, ¾ in. x 1½ in.

2¾ in.

1 in.

Solid mahogany backing inset into plywood core

2½ in.

¾ in.

Mortise, ⅛ in. deep, accepts support stand.

Writing surfaces, ⅜ in. x 9¾ in. x 14⅜ in., are made of ¼-in. plywood and covered on both sides with 1⁄16-in.-thick mahogany veneer.

Cleat, 5⁄16 in. by 9⁄16 in. x 10½ in., is screwed into place with brass flathead screws.

13⁄16 in.

½ in.

Veneer covers end-grain banding, then the entire edge is rounded over.

1¼ in.

¾ in.

4½ in.

2¾ in.

1¼ in.

¾ in.

4 in.

½ in.

12¾ n.

A STAND THAT FOLDS AWAY. The top of the desk is mortised to accept the support stand, which is hinged to the lower writing surface.

entirely hidden in the rabbet. I cut solid mahogany spline material so that the grain runs the same direction as the sides of the carcase, allowing for expansion and contraction all in the same direction and at the same rate.

Assembling the carcase–Because the plywood-core panels minimize wood movement, you can glue the top and bottom to the sides of the carcase. If you're using solid wood panels, I would suggest that you use just small brads without glue; this will allow the wood to move just a bit and should keep the desk from tearing itself apart.

Glue up the carcase first, then fit the drawer to the opening. Be sure the carcase is flat when you glue it up. Either set it on a flat surface or use winding sticks on the surface to sight along the top surfaces.

DELICATE DOVETAILS AND MORE

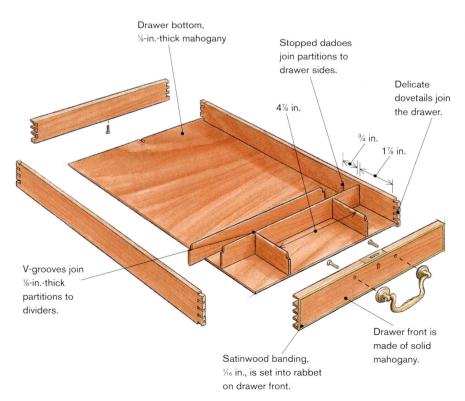

Drawer bottom, ⅛-in.-thick mahogany

Stopped dadoes join partitions to drawer sides.

Delicate dovetails join the drawer.

4⅞ in.

¾ in.

1⅞ in.

V-grooves join ⅛-in.-thick partitions to dividers.

Satinwood banding, ¹⁄₁₆ in., is set into rabbet on drawer front.

Drawer front is made of solid mahogany.

It's a Challenge to Build and Fit the Drawer

The drawer in the original is a traditional, dovetailed box with a solid wood bottom. It's an especially challenging job, just as it must have been then, because the sides and partitions are so thin—³⁄₁₆ in. for the sides and ⅛ in. for the partitions.

Start by fitting the drawer sides and front into the carcase, allowing for a bit of expansion over time. The dovetails in this drawer are so small that even a ⅛-in. chisel is too large. (I ground an old chisel down to a little less than ³⁄₃₂ in. for the job.) Lay out and cut the dovetails, fit the bottom of the drawer into a groove, and tackle the partitions last.

The thin drawer partitions are held in place with V-grooves and mitered points, which act as tenons. These are easier to cut than you might think. Mitered points can be cut on a miter saw, and the grooves are easily made on the tablesaw with a crosscut sled and the blade set at 45°.

A Delicate Touch to Make and Install the Support Stand

Made of ⅛-in.-thick material, the support stand is a very delicate assembly. Cut out the pieces and run the half-lap joints and hinge mortises on the tablesaw crosscut sled, then smooth the cuts with a scraper.

To help guide the laminate trimmer, use a simple jig consisting of a small piece of plywood with a straightedge glued along one face. With the small straight bit in the laminate trimmer, trim the jig so that its edge is at the edge of the cut. With this jig, the bit cuts exactly along the edge of the plywood. It's easy to clamp the jig along the pencil line, starting and stopping the cut as needed. The round corners of the mortise can be squared up with a chisel.

DETAILING THE DRAWER. Satinwood banding is applied to a small rabbet on the drawer front. Tape holds the banding in place until the glue dries.

SLICE AND REJOIN VENEER. On the back carcase panel, instead of inlaying the satinwood stringing, approach it as a marquetry project. Use a small knife to cut the veneer into sections.

This Small Desk Takes a Lot of Hardware

For such a small piece, there is a considerable amount of hardware to mount—six hinges, a mortised lock, and the handle. You can mortise for all of the hinges at one time, using the same straight router bit you used to cut mortises for the support stand. Then square up the corners and trim the edges with a knife and chisel.

To find the depth for the hinge mortises fastening the bottom writing surface to the carcase, hold the hinge leaves closed but parallel. Half of this measurement, not the thickness of the leaf, is the right depth for this hinge mortise. For the other hinges—fastening the support stand and holding the upper writing surface to the lower one—only mortise to the depth of the hinge-leaf thickness itself.

The hinges used in this project need very small screws. But wood screws, even small ones, have a smooth shank, then taper from there to the end of the screw. This means that there are only very shallow threads for the lower ⅛ in. To make matters worse, the support stand is only ⅛ in., so it's impossible to use conventional wood screws to mount the hinges. Though unconventional, I used solid-brass, slotted machine screws (#2 by 56 tpi by ¼ in. long). First drill ¹⁄₁₆-in. pilot holes, then use an awl to enlarge the holes slightly. The machine screws have a remarkable amount of holding power, even in the thin support stand. I shortened the screws for the support stand by holding them with pliers against the grinding wheel of a bench grinder.

The lock mortise is pretty straightforward to cut with a router and chisels. Just make sure that you cut the mortise for the lock and drill for the drawer pull before you assemble the drawer.

Antiquing the hardware–The drawer pull came polished, the hinges came plain, and the mortise lock was brushed. I wanted it all to look the same, so I decided to antique all of the brass. I soaked the hardware in lacquer thinner to take off the lacquer, then used Brass Darkening Solution from Crown City Hardware (626-794-1188) to make everything the same color. It took only about 30 minutes and worked amazingly well, leaving everything a uniform dark brown. By polishing slightly with 0000

Only about the size of a stack of legal pads, this project combines traditional joinery with modern tools.

Miters and Rabbets Join the Carcase

SPLINED MITER CUTS. The carcase is assembled with miters and reinforced with splines. With the ends of the stock cut to 45°, the spline slots can be cut on the crosscut sled at the tablesaw. To allow for uniform expansion, cut spline material to fit with the grain going the same direction as the sides of the carcase.

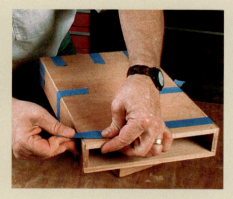

TAPE UP THE MITERED CARCASE JOINERY. Tape helps hold the joints in place before the clamps go on. After applying tape to the outside of the mitered joints, flip the assembly and coat the mitered ends with glue.

or synthetic steel wool, you can bring the surface finish back up to whatever polish you like.

After all of the hardware is in place and adjusted, remove it to sand and finish the entire project.

An Ideal Finish for the Laptop

Though you can just as easily scrape, plane, or sand the surfaces of this laptop for finishing, I sanded by machine during the building process with a belt sander and 120-grit paper, then sanded by hand using a felt block with 120 grit, and then with 150 and 220 grit.

The finish for the desk should have a satin sheen—not too glossy and not too dull. All you need to get a nice, durable, hand-rubbed finish is high-gloss spar varnish, thinner (I used turpentine), 400-grit wet-or-dry sandpaper, some rags, and a little elbow grease. Simply rubbing gloss varnish onto the raw wood, then wiping off the excess with a rag will provide the protection and sheen that closely match the 225-year-old original, not the glossy sheen you'd expect from a high-gloss varnish. Gloss works best as a wipe-on finish because it has greater clarity and will not hide the wood grain as a semigloss or eggshell finish would.

Wearing gloves and using the wet-or-dry sandpaper, rub all of the surfaces with varnish thinned by one-third. Cover the entire surface and sand until you produce a slurry, which acts as a pore filler.

With the varnish still wet, wipe the surface with a soft cotton rag and buff until the surface is slick and smooth. Polish again with a clean, dry cloth after a few minutes to make sure no wet spots remain. The next day, lightly sand it dry with 320-grit paper. Repeat the process with unthinned varnish each day until you build up three or four coats. Each coat will produce slightly more luster. Rubbing gloss varnish this way produces a lovely hand-rubbed sheen that's hard to beat.

Applying the Baize Can be Tricky

The cloth used on the writing surface looks a lot like felt, but it's actually a woven fabric. It's called baize and is available in a wide range of colors from billiard supply houses. Make sure you mark the back of the cloth.

Apply the cloth to the writing surface after the finish has been applied and the hinges are in place but before mounting the book stop. This way the top and bottom writing surfaces can be laid out flat on the bench.

Using blue masking tape, carefully mask off a wood border of about ½ in. around the cloth, then cut out a piece of cloth about 1 in. oversized. I used 3M Super 77 spray adhesive in an aerosol can, applying the adhesive to both the writing surface and the back of the cloth. Use only a light coat on the fabric so that the adhesive doesn't bleed through. After about 30 seconds of drying

ASSEMBLING THE CARCASE.
Once glue is applied to all the joints, tape helps hold the carcase assembly in place. Once the assembly is clamped up, use winding sticks to check the flatness.

time, begin laying the cloth onto the working surface, smoothing out the wrinkles as you go.

Now comes the tricky part. Using a razor-sharp utility knife and a straightedge, carefully trim the cloth to size, trying not to cut too deeply into the wood but making sure you cut all the way through the fabric. As the cuts are made, pull up the extra fabric and masking tape.

Only about the size of a stack of legal pads, this project combines traditional joinery with modern tools, materials, and techniques, resulting in a replica of the lovely little writing desk that played such a large part in U.S. political history—a "Relic of Revolution," indeed.

LON SCHLEINING sells full-sized plans of this project on his Web site: www.woodbender.com. He is the author of *Treasure Chests: The Legacy of Extraordinary Boxes* and *The Workbench: A Complete Guide to Creating Your Perfect Bench.*

Splined Miters Join Mirror Frame

BY BOB GLEASON

As a luthier living in Hawaii, I have the opportunity to work with beautiful, exotic woods. With today's environmental concerns, I've learned to use these species efficiently. For example, with the small, narrow stock left-overs I accumulate, I do short production runs of special projects. One of these is a small version of a cheval mirror (see the photos on p. 52), which is relatively quick to build and is an attractive addition to a tabletop or desktop.

The mirror pivots in a stand that consists of two sides (feet attached to uprights) connected by a stretcher, as shown in figure 1. A pair of knobs at the pivot point enable the mirror to be fixed at different angles. A mitered back frame retains two wooden panels in a recess at the back of the frame. The mirror frame itself is mitered and splined, and because these corner joints are exposed and tricky to cut cleanly, I built a jig that lets me quickly and consistently cut grooves for the splines. The jig (see Figure 2 on the facing page) is made of plywood and has runners that slide in my tablesaw's miter slots.

Picking and Preparing Stock

I try to pick out matching wood for the mirror's frame and stand parts, preferably using 8/4 stock, so I can resaw it to book-match pieces. For the adjustment knobs, I cut out two ¾-in.-sq. by 2-in.-long blanks. For the accent plugs and splines, I use ebony or rosewood (my fingerboard remnants). I thickness the frame and stand pieces to ⅞ in. Then I surface the two back panels and the back-frame pieces to ⅛ in. thick. Next, I rip the frame stock into 1½-in. strips. I leave the strips long rather than crosscutting them to length. Finally, I use a ⅜-in. roundover bit to ease the strip's edges except for what will be the frame's outside corners.

Cutting the Frame's Rabbet, Miters, and Grooves

Because I often work with figured woods that chip out easily, I like to use my table-saw when rabbeting the frame instead of using a shaper or router. The frame's rabbet receives both the ¼-in.-thick mirror glass and the back panels. Cut the rabbet ⅝ in. wide, so you won't see the cut edge of the glass when viewing the mirror from an angle. Next, miter the frame's corners accurately because the frame will be viewed often and from a close distance. After the glue is dry, smooth the joints flush. Then, using a table-saw jig like the one shown in Figure 2, cut slots for each of the corner splines.

MIRROR AND STAND ASSEMBLY

Construct the frame first. If needed, alter the stand to fit the frame. Position the pivot more than halfway up the frame. For more stability, use ¼-in.-instead of ⅛-in.-thick mirror glass.

GROOVING JIG FOR CORNER SPLINES

Adjust stops to hold frame vertically and edge-centered with the tablesaw blade. All parts are ⅝-in. plywood unless otherwise noted.

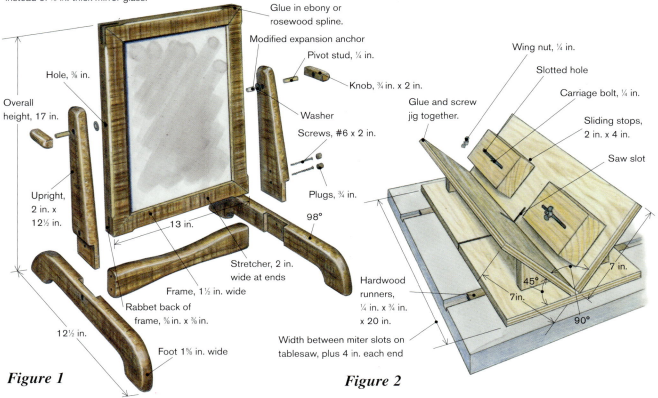

Glue in ebony or rosewood spline.

Modified expansion anchor

Pivot stud, ¼ in.

Knob, ¾ in. x 2 in.

Washer

Screws, #6 x 2 in.

Plugs, ¾ in.

98°

Hole, ⅜ in.

Overall height, 17 in.

Upright, 2 in. x 12½ in.

13 in.

Stretcher, 2 in. wide at ends

Frame, 1½ in. wide

Rabbet back of frame, ⅝ in. x ⅜ in.

12½ in.

Foot 1⅝ in. wide

Hardwood runners, ¼ in. x ¾ in. x 20 in.

Width between miter slots on tablesaw, plus 4 in. each end

Wing nut, ¼ in.

Slotted hole

Carriage bolt, ¼ in.

Glue and screw jig together.

Sliding stops, 2 in. x 4 in.

Saw slot

45°

7in.

7 in.

90°

Figure 1

Figure 2

Installing the Mirror and Back

The mating edges of the two back panels are beveled so that one or both of them can expand or contract. To hide the joint and to flush up the panels, insert dark construction paper between the mirror and the panels (unless your mirror already has a dark backing). Next, roundover the edges of the back-frame pieces. To join the back-frame miters, lay out the frame flat and perfectly square on waxed paper. Then, with cyanoacrylate (super) glue, bond the corners together one at a time. So that the glass can be readily exchanged, drill slightly oversized holes in the back frame for ½-in.-long, 16d brass escutcheon pins (see the right photo on p. 52). Drill slightly undersized holes in the mirror frame, install the panels and back frame, and then drive the pins home.

Assembling the Stand

Appropriately, the two sides of the stand are mirror images. To cut the half-lap joints in each foot and upright, slant your miter gauge 8° to the left for the right leg and 8° to the right for the left leg. Once you've wasted exactly half the wood thickness between the layout lines using multiple saw passes, clean up the joint with a sharp chisel and a hard sanding block. Before you glue up the sides, bandsaw the tapered shape of the uprights and the curve of the feet. Then sand the edges that will be joined. When the glued-up sides are set, round over the edges with a router, and thoroughly sand both sides.

When you bandsaw the stretcher's profile, remember that its width must clear the pivoting mirror. The length of the stretcher is also critical. If it's too short, the problem

WHEN MAKING TILTING TABLE-TOP MIRRORS, the author uses exotic-wood leftovers from his guitarmaking business. The mirror's design, a small version of a cheval mirror, relies on smooth forms for the components and contrasting woods for the exposed joinery.

BECAUSE THIS FIDDLEBACK KOA and ebony mirror will be touched often, Gleason finished the wood with lacquer, which is easy to clean. The mitered back frame, held with brass pins, retains the floating panels.

is obvious. If it's too long, the tips of the uprights will tilt inward and touch the mirror frame when the knobs are tightened. In addition, the ends of the stretcher must be cut at exactly 90°, or the stand will be askew. Allow ¼ in. extra length for brass washers and for the adjustment knobs to work properly. Position the stretcher in the same plane as the slant of the uprights; one screw goes through the upright and the other goes through the foot. Butt join and cap the stretcher to each side using glue, screws (#6 by 2 in.), and ⅜-in.-dia. plugs.

Mounting the Frame on Pivot Studs

I use ¼-in. threaded rod for the mirror's pivot studs. One stud attaches to the back of each knob. Drill a hole two-thirds of the way through the back center of each knob. The stud length equals the depth of the hole, the thickness of the upright, two washers, and ⅜ in. to go into the frame. Cut the rod to this length, bevel one end so that it threads easily into a ¼-in. nut, and then epoxy the stud's other end perpendicular to the knob's back.

To screw the knob studs into the mirror frame, you could install threaded inserts, but I just use ¼-in. expansion anchors that are carried by most hardware stores. Punch out the spreader slug on the back of each anchor, remove the little ball, and grind off the end until the anchor is ½ in. long. Next, mark the pivot points on the sides of the frame 8½ in. up from the bottom. After clamping a temporary stop across the back of the uprights, place a ⅛-in. shim on top of the stretcher and set the mirror in place. Carefully transfer the frame's pivot marks to the uprights. After you've bored ⅜-in. holes through the center of the uprights, place the frame back on the shim on the stand. With a brad-point bit, re-mark the frame's pivot stud holes through the holes in the uprights. Finally, drill ⅜-in. holes in the frame edges and epoxy the modified anchors in them. After you've sealed all the wood (I use lacquer), mount the mirror to its stand with the screw knobs.

BOB GLEASON builds custom guitars and ukuleles in Hilo, Hawaii.

Picture-Framing Techniques

BY LEON SEGAL

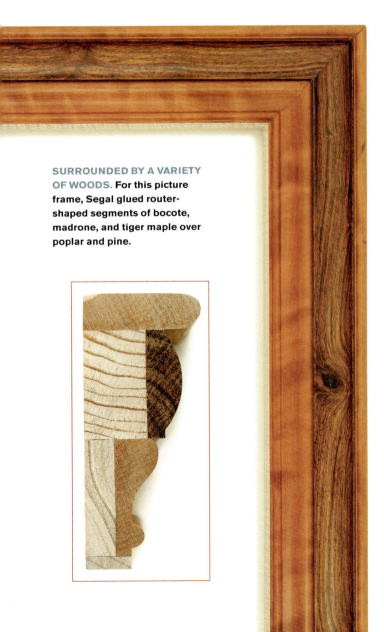

SURROUNDED BY A VARIETY OF WOODS. For this picture frame, Segal glued router-shaped segments of bocote, madrone, and tiger maple over poplar and pine.

I started making frames for my family's paintings and photographs because I was unimpressed by the cheap pressed-wood frames I'd seen in department stores. Once I decided to make my picture frames from exotic and domestic hardwoods, I quickly found that no matter what type of frame I built—whether a simple solid frame or a built-up frame like the one in the photo on this page—I could use my shopmade router table to perform 90 percent of the work and achieve high quality. The router does a fine job shaping the outside of a frame (see the top photo on p. 54) and rabbeting for a picture and glass. With special fences and jigs, the router also neatly plows grooves for miter splines and for a slide-in back.

Design and Materials

I often vary a frame's design to suit a picture. Although most of the differences are in the frame profile and decorative treatment, I've also tried variations in the construction of the frames. For example, if I need to frame a large portrait that necessitates a wide frame, I combine several profiles in the frame, such as coves, flutes, and ogees (see the photo at left). Using individ-

53

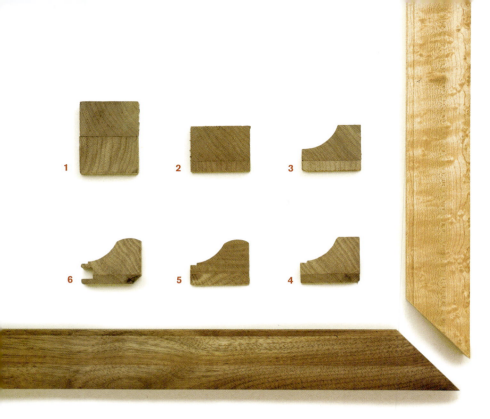

THE TWO HARDWOOD FRAME PIECES are identical in profile, and each will accept a simple, applied back. But the bird's-eye maple piece (right) looks lively while the dark walnut piece (bottom) appears more formal. The six cross sections show the shaping sequence Segal used (clockwise from top left): After glue-up (1), he ripped down the stock (2). Then, using his router table, he cut the cove, rabbet, roundover, groove, and chamfer (3 through 6).

ual sections can give depth to a frame, and it allows me to save precious species of wood for the visible parts. I use less valuable woods for the unseen fill areas.

Before I make a frame, I usually sketch a profile and note any critical dimensions. I can still refine details and proportions later, but the sketch helps me to choose the woods to use and to figure approximately how much of each kind I will need. Depending on the hardwood that I select, I can give a frame a light look or a more formal appearance (see the photo above), and I can even pick woods that will complement the colors in the picture to be framed. If I'm gluing up a frame, I often prepare contrasting woods, being sure to plane surfaces that will be mated. To minimize bow in the stock, I first rough-crosscut the long pieces in two. Then I joint the sections square.

Decorative inlays are my favorite border for frames. I make my own inlay bandings ⅛ in. to ¼ in. thick, which allows enough

depth for router-shaping (see the photo on p. 55). I save cutoffs and frame scraps to make refrigerator magnets or key chains.

Shaping and Assembling

Although I frequently build up thicknesses to make a frame, gluelines are seldom a problem. They can be virtually invisible if located below the rabbet that will hold the picture. On the outside of a frame, you can rout a bevel or cove to disguise the line (see the drawing on p. 56), which also helps remove frame bulk.

To rout a shape, a ¼-in.-radius cove for example, I take several passes on the router table, plus a light (under ¼ in.) finishing pass. This reduces tearout, especially on highly figured stock. Straight-grained stock will usually rout cleanly, but even so, I always move the work slowly. I form the rest of the profile with a sequence of router shaping (see the photo at left). To make the operations safe and fast, I use several router-

RELYING ON HIS SHOPMADE ROUTER TABLE for shaping work, Segal advances an assembled frame by the bit, taking multiple passes. He uses a custom-made fence with an appropriately sized cutout for the bit.

table fences with hold-downs dedicated to special tasks. Each one is different in height or has a cutout sized for a particular bit.

To form a recess for the picture, mat, and glass, I use a straight bit and plow a ¼-in.-deep rabbet in the inside of the frame. The rabbet's width depends on the size of the picture. I allow ½ in. clearance, so everything slides in easily. The back-holding slot can be cut in the frame itself or in a rail attached to the back (see the drawing on p. 57). I leave a ⅛-in.-thick lip on the back for strength. If I use a back rail, I glue it to the frame after I've routed the other profiles.

WITH A GROOVE-CUTTING JIG AND A SLOT-CUTTER in his router table, Segal plows grooves in this inlaid frame for the miter splines. The jig cradles the frame corner securely at a 45° angle to the fence and keeps his hands out of harm's way.

Frames from Recycled Moldings

MARKING AND CLAMPING MITERS. Ted Myers made two fixtures to help him make frames from salvaged moldings.

As a certified Yankee, it grieves me to see architectural remnants wasted. Scraps of molding from doors and windows or narrow boards often wind up in a wood stove or at a landfill. Because of a few nails, a lack of breadth, old paint, or a knot here or there, these castoffs are sadly condemned to oblivion. I can't bear to see that happen, so I've been back-logging old moldings to make picture frames.

It's fairly easy to strip off layers of paint and to fill nail holes and cracks. Old moldings can be left with their original patina, or, once sanded, they can be waxed, painted, stained, or varnished. Leftover barn wood, colored by Mother Nature, also makes a handsome frame. If I don't like a piece's profile, I reshape it using handplanes or my router.

To help construct frames, I made two devices: a miter-marking gauge and a clamping fixture (see the photo at left). The gauge lets me accurately transfer a cutoff line that I've marked on the inside of the rabbet for the picture. To make the gauge, I first cut the right-triangle base from a scrap of 1x4 pine. Then I made the sides from lauan, sawing out the molding windows using a Dremel tool.

The clamping fixture has two fixed stops and two adjustable angle brackets that pivot. Cutouts in the bottom legs of the bracket accept dogs with ¼-20 by 2-in. machine screws that clamp the frame on the particleboard base.

With framed pictures now filling up my family's wall spaces (my stock of moldings greatly reduced), I justifiably took two buckets of 2 in.-long scraps toward the kindling pile. But then I thought: "Why not glue them to that plywood scrap that blew off that fellow's pickup truck—spray it all white—enter it as a piece of sculpture at the next East Grandy Arts-N-Crafts Show? Now where is that glue bottle?"

A Mitering Fixture

The mitering fixture sits on the saw's table and butts against the rear crosscutting fence. The fixture has two fences screwed to a plywood auxiliary table. But unlike that setup, my device enables exact miters at any point in a piece of stock—an important feature if you want to cut a miter near the center of a long section.

I can align long work against either miter fence without the piece interfering with the normal fence. This also allows the waste to fall safely in back of the crosscutting fence. The different heights of the fences let me miter either left- or right-handed. I just shim the work with a block of appropriate thickness so that the workpiece clears the opposite fence.

When you're screwing down the lower fence, countersink the heads, so they won't interfere with the work when you're aligning a piece against the right fence. And when you're shimming work with plywood or other stock, raise the blade, so it just cuts through the workpiece. If the work tends to slip when supported against the exposed height of the fence, stick some 220-grit sandpaper to the registration surface using double-faced tape.

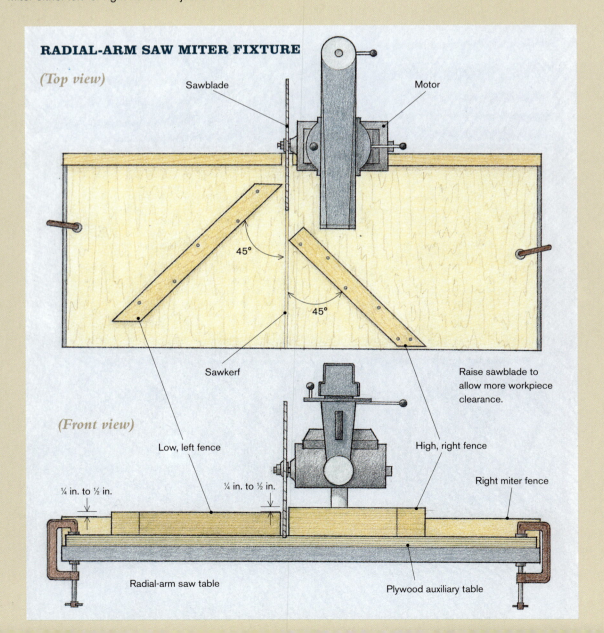

RADIAL-ARM SAW MITER FIXTURE

(Top view)

Sawblade

Motor

45°

45°

Sawkerf

Raise sawblade to allow more workpiece clearance.

(Front view)

Low, left fence

High, right fence

Right miter fence

¼ in. to ½ in.

¼ in. to ½ in.

Radial-arm saw table

Plywood auxiliary table

Mitering and prefinishing parts–You can build frames from single moldings (see the sidebar on the facing page), or you can build up a frame from sections and then tilt the frame slightly. This requires the miters to be cut at compound angles. However, I prefer to make nontilted frames, so I can leave the work flat and cut the miters at 45°. The perception of depth is achieved by the profiles I routed.

Before I cut any miters, I apply a thinned coat of varnish to the pieces. The prefinish keeps glue stains off the mitered corners, and the thinner prevents the saw-blade and router bits from gumming up. I cut the frame miters on my radial-arm saw using a fixture (see the box on the facing page). The wider the frame, the more important the accuracy of the miter. I first miter the long sides of a frame. If I cut a long piece short or if too much tearout occurs, I can almost always cut the shorter section from this longer piece.

Cutting and inserting splines–I usually reinforce my miters by inserting visible corner splines. With the frame glued together, I rout the spline grooves using a slot-cutting bit and the jig shown in the photo at right. I cut the splines from contrasting wood, leaving them oversized, so I can trim them flush after the glue is dry.

I orient the grain of the splines at 45°, which means the outside corner is the weakest point, the spot where routing tearout is likely to occur (see the splined miter detail above left). Therefore, I make sure the spline and its groove have adequate glue near the point, and I take extra care when trimming the corner. By shaping the underside of the frame, you can reveal more of the spline as a decorative touch (see the photo on p. 58).

Making and fitting the back–How you treat the back of the frame depends on whether you want the picture to hang on a wall or stand on a table. For a wall-hung

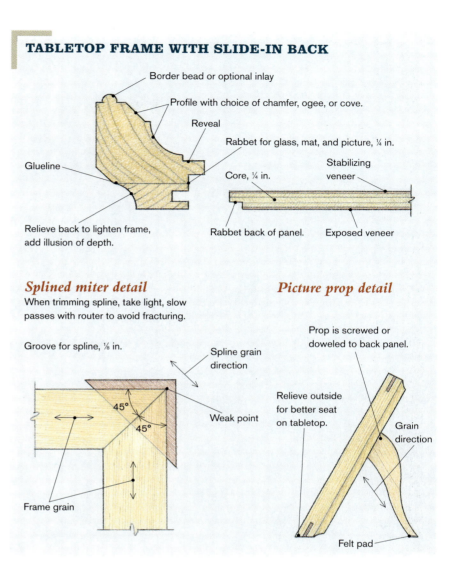

TABLETOP FRAME WITH SLIDE-IN BACK

Border bead or optional inlay

Profile with choice of chamfer, ogee, or cove.

Reveal

Rabbet for glass, mat, and picture, ¼ in.

Glueline

Core, ¼ in.

Stabilizing veneer

Relieve back to lighten frame, add illusion of depth.

Rabbet back of panel.

Exposed veneer

Splined miter detail
When trimming spline, take light, slow passes with router to avoid fracturing.

Groove for spline, ⅛ in.

Spline grain direction

45°

45°

Weak point

Frame grain

Picture prop detail

Prop is screwed or doweled to back panel.

Relieve outside for better seat on tabletop.

Grain direction

Felt pad

frame, you can install a cardboard or plywood back with turn-buttons to hold the picture in place. For a standing frame, I like to put on a sliding back, so there won't be any exposed hardware.

To make a decorative back panel, I veneer both sides of a plywood core (see the drawing above). For the core, I use ⅛-in. (3-ply) poplar plywood or ¼-in. lauan. After I glue on the veneers, I cut the back panel about ½ in. wider than the opening width in the back of the frame. Next I cut the panel 1 in. longer than the opening, so it extends past the frame contents. Then I rout a rabbet on the sides and top of the back so that it slides into the groove in the back (or back rail) of the frame.

ACCESS SLOT. After routing a picture-entry slot by sliding this frame between two stop blocks on his router table, Segal checks the fit of the glass. The frame back was coved to show more of the spline.

Installing the picture—To slide in the picture, glass, mat, and back, there must be an entry slot. After the frame is assembled, I rout an access slot in the frame's bottom, where it will be inconspicuous. To set the width of the cut, I clamp on a pair of stop blocks to the router-table fence: one block to start the cut (see the photo above), one to end it. With a ½-in. spiral bit positioned adjacent to the router table's fence, I move the frame left and right between the stops and make the slot in multiple passes. Then I use a chisel and sandpaper to trim and smooth the routed area.

If you lift a standing frame from a table, you don't want the sliding back to fall out. So I insert cardboard spacers to form a friction fit between the picture and the back. If I'm not using a mat, I just insert more cardboard. After I have fit the picture, I mark and cut the back to final length.

Other back details—When a frame is destined for a table or desk, I give it a simple prop to support the frame upright (see the picture prop detail on p. 57). I make the prop from scrapwood, sometimes laminating together a few pieces. By installing the prop to the back with a single fastener, I make the prop swivel, so the picture can stand either vertically or horizontally. You may have to vary the length of the leg, the angle of the frame, or the attachment location to get the frame to sit the way you want. And you may want to relieve some more of the frame bottom, so it sits more comfortably on the tabletop.

LEON SEGAL is a business manager and woodworker in Randolph, N.J.

A Basic Mirror Frame Detailed to Your Liking

BY D. DOUGLAS
MOOBERRY

Mirrors make great wedding presents. You can make them as small or as large as you like, depending on how generous you're feeling. Mirrors don't require a lot of material or time, either. I learned that in college, when I needed to come up with gifts and a little spending money.

After I graduated from college and was unable to find a business that wanted to make me president, I started making mirrors full time. Then other furniture projects came along, and mirrors got put on the sidelines, until I hired an apprentice.

Although I build Chippendale-style mirrors, the basic construction techniques are applicable to any style mirror, with or without fretwork. Actually, you could use these techniques to build picture frames,

THE KEY TO A STRONG MITER JOINT. The author cuts slots for splines in all four corners of a mirror frame.

Shaping the Molding

With a little creativity, you can mix and match stock router bits to create interesting moldings.

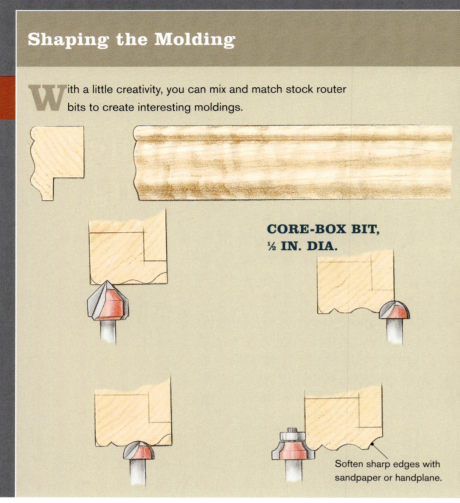

CORE-BOX BIT, ½ IN. DIA.

Soften sharp edges with sandpaper or handplane.

SHAPE THE FRAME. Start with wide stock. When using multiple router bits, sketch the molding profile before beginning.

CUT A RABBET FOR THE GLASS AND BACK PANEL. After the molding is machined and ripped to width, cut a rabbet ⅜ in. wide by ½ in. deep.

too. Best of all, you don't even need clamps to assemble them.

Fretwork Pattern Is Up to You

Copying an existing mirror is the easiest way to get a design. My mirror is a copy of one owned by my mother. Trace the design onto plain paper. Then go back with your pencil to refine any ragged curves. The fretwork on old mirrors usually looks symmetrical, but often it's not.

If you trace the fretwork from an old mirror, copy one-half of the design, or you can use mine (see the drawing on p. 62). When copying it onto a workpiece, use both sides of the pattern for a mirror image. If you plan to make only one mirror, tape the design to the wood and cut away.

For repeatability, make reusable templates out of scrap laminate or fiberboard.

If you don't have a mirror to copy, look in books and magazines. When you find a picture you like, blow it up on a photocopier to the desired size. Or use an existing design and modify it. Use ears from one design on another. But don't take away too many details, or you risk making something bland. Old mirrors have lots of details, lots of curves, little points, and frills. Don't make your mirror look like it was made at a factory with a pin router and a ¼-in. bit.

Select Straighter-Grained Stock for the Frame

Heavily figured woods, such as tiger or bird's-eye maple, are prone to movement, and that can give you fits if the frame starts warping. In any given board, there are usually sections of greater and lesser figure. Use the less-figured areas for the frame and the highly figured stock for the fretwork.

I try to keep a distance between my fingers and things that can cut them off. That's why I run molding using large stock whenever possible (see the top photo on the facing page). Molding can be cut with a variety of router bits to get a specific shape (see the drawings on the facing page). Or you may find one bit that gives you just what you want in a single pass. You're the designer, and you don't have to be a slave to someone else's ideas. There are many ways to shape a pleasing molding.

I use 1¼-in.-thick stock for the frame, and I shape the profile on the router table or shaper. When using various router bits to create a custom molding, draw out the profile on the edge of a board for a visual aid. Chuck in the first bit, make the necessary adjustments, and mill all the stock the same way. Then set up the second bit and do the same. This method not only saves you time, but it ensures that the molding will match. One rule of woodworking is that every time you run molding, it comes out slightly different.

Next, rip the molding ⅞ in. wide on the tablesaw. Then return to the router table and cut the rabbet on the back of the frame using a straight bit or rabbeting bit (see the bottom photo on the facing page). The rabbet must be deep enough to hold the mirror glass and back panel. Don't forget to leave some room for the nails. I make my rabbets ⅜ in. wide by ½ in. deep.

Splined Miters Join the Frame

There are many ways to cut miters, but I prefer a chop saw. I set up a simple fence on the saw—just a ¾-in. by 3-in. by 3-ft. scrap that allows me to set up a length stop. It's very important that the miter be exactly 45°. The graduations on a chop saw aren't

Construction of a Mirror

A VIEW FROM THE BACK
The glass and back panel fit into a rabbet cut into the rear of the frame.

INSTALL AN AUXILIARY FENCE on the miter saw to prevent tearout. Cut the molded frame pieces to size, then glue and clamp the mitered corners (packing tape works well). When dry, cut slots for the corner splines on the tablesaw with a V-jig. Glue the splines into the slots, then cut off the excess when the glue has set.

Splines secure a miter-joined frame.

Dressing Up a Mirror Frame with Fretwork

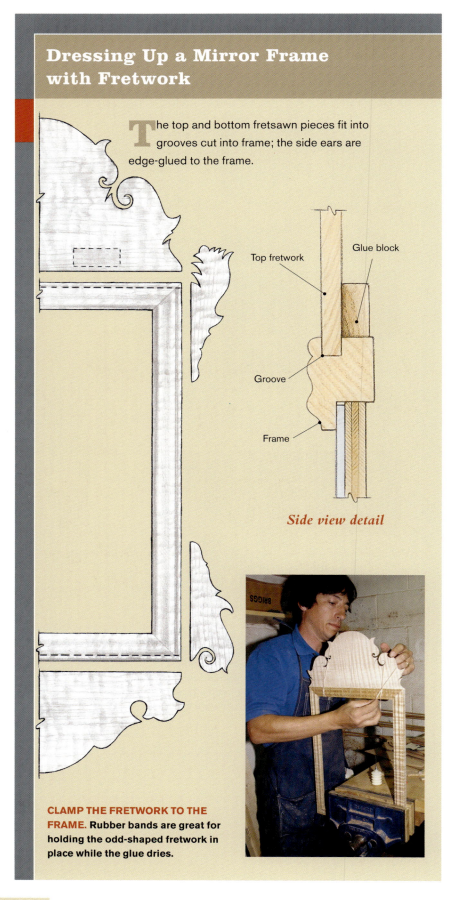

The top and bottom fretsawn pieces fit into grooves cut into frame; the side ears are edge-glued to the frame.

Glue block

Top fretwork

Groove

Frame

Side view detail

CLAMP THE FRETWORK TO THE FRAME. Rubber bands are great for holding the odd-shaped fretwork in place while the glue dries.

always accurate; check your settings by cutting and fitting some scrap.

Now it's time for the real fun: sanding the molding. It is much easier to sand the molding before the frame is assembled. The better your tooling, the less you have to sand. I like clear packing tape (the kind that stretches) better than fancy clamps for joining miters and other joints. To assemble the frame, dab a little yellow glue on the mating surfaces of a miter, then wrap the two pieces tightly with tape. Put the whole frame together this way in one session, and make adjustments to all the miters as you glue up so that all the joints are tight. The larger the frame, the easier it goes together because it will flex to conform.

After the glue has dried, remove the tape and cut the grooves for the corner splines to reinforce the frame. I cut the grooves on a tablesaw using a simple V-jig (see the photo on p. 59). The jig holds the frame at a 45° angle and safely guides it through a standard ⅛ in. kerf blade, cutting about 1 in. deep into each corner.

I plane spline stock, of the same wood as the frame, to ⅛ in. thick. Glue these strips into each corner (see the bottom photo on p. 61). Once the glue has set, cut off the excess and sand or plane the joints smooth. Now cut a shallow dado into the top and bottom edges of the frame to hold the fretwork. (The side pieces are just edge-glued to the frame.)

Use a Scroll Saw for the Fretwork

Trace or tape your design for the fretwork onto stock that's been resawn to ¼ in. thick. Be sure to align the fretwork stock so that the grain runs in the same direction as the frame. In other words, the grain on the horizontal pieces runs left to right; the grain on the vertical fretwork runs up and down. Before starting, look over your stock and make sure the edges that attach to the frame are jointed before cutting out the patterns. It's very difficult to true up the edges of little pieces.

I use a variable-speed scroll saw and a fine-tooth blade to cut the fretwork. Many of the newer scroll saws, those that keep the blade under constant tension, cut very smoothly. If you cut right to the line with a fluid motion, you end up with cutouts that require very little sanding and filing.

After the fretwork is cut out, clean up any rough edges and sand the pieces up to 220-grit. Next, glue the fretwork to the frame using rubber bands for clamps (see the photo on the facing page). I suggest gluing up one side at a time. If you try to do the entire mirror, you're likely to misalign a just-completed section while banding together another. For reinforcement, add glue blocks between the fretwork and frame on the back.

The top and bottom cutouts fit into ¼-in.-deep grooves cut in the frame. I size these two pieces slightly wider than the frame. After glue-up, I trim them with a chisel; that makes a snug fit to the ears. After another go-around with sanding, I finish the mirror with aniline stains and then shellac. When it's dry, I rub it out with steel wool and apply a couple of coats of paste wax. I like to finish both sides of the frame.

It's best to order the mirror glass after you've glued up the frame (see the box above), just in case your plan dimensions have strayed from the actual piece. Cut the frame back out of ¼-in. stock or plywood; size it for a snug fit. A good-fitting back will cover up a loose-fitting mirror.

If you want to have some fun, stick an old newspaper between the mirror and the back before assembling it. Fifty years from now, the person who replaces the mirror will appreciate the old headlines.

The mirror and back are held in place with brads partially nailed into the frame's rabbet. I use a nail gun because it's faster than predrilling little holes and then carefully tapping away at tiny nails with a hammer. Ironically, the brads from an air nailer look much like the handmade square-cut nails from Tremont Nail Co.

Finish by attaching a pair of picture hangers to the back, and string a piece of stranded wire between them.

D. DOUGLAS MOOBERRY builds custom and reproduction furniture in Unionville, Pa.

It's best to order the mirror glass after you've glued up the frame.

Pear Mantel Clock

BY MARIO RODRIGUEZ

My daughter Isabel's seventh birthday was fast approaching, and I wanted to build her something special. She had recently learned to tell time, so a clock seemed like the perfect way to mark the occasion. I designed the clock in the Arts-and-Crafts style; it looks somewhat contemporary but still has a traditional feel (see the photo at left). The joinery is simple, just stub tenons and dadoes, most of which can be cut quickly on a router table and tablesaw.

The clock consists of eight parts: the top, bottom, and two sides, the middle shelf assembly, veneered panels for the face and back of the clock, and a door below the middle shelf. The clock is just a bit taller than 16 in. As a result, not a lot of wood is required to build it, and the planing, sanding, and finishing don't take very long.

This clock is made of pear, which has a very mild grain that lets the clock's design dominate. A coursely grained or heavily figured wood could overpower a clock of this size.

CLEAN LINES AND FEW DETAILS make this clock handsome and easy to build.

PEAR MANTEL CLOCK

Grooves and dadoes on the underside of the clock top accept tenons from the sides and the face and back panels.

Simple joinery makes this small clock a quick build. Dadoes are ¼ in. wide and ¼ in. deep. Grooves for face panel and back panel are slightly wider to accept ¼-in. plywood panels that have been veneered on one side.

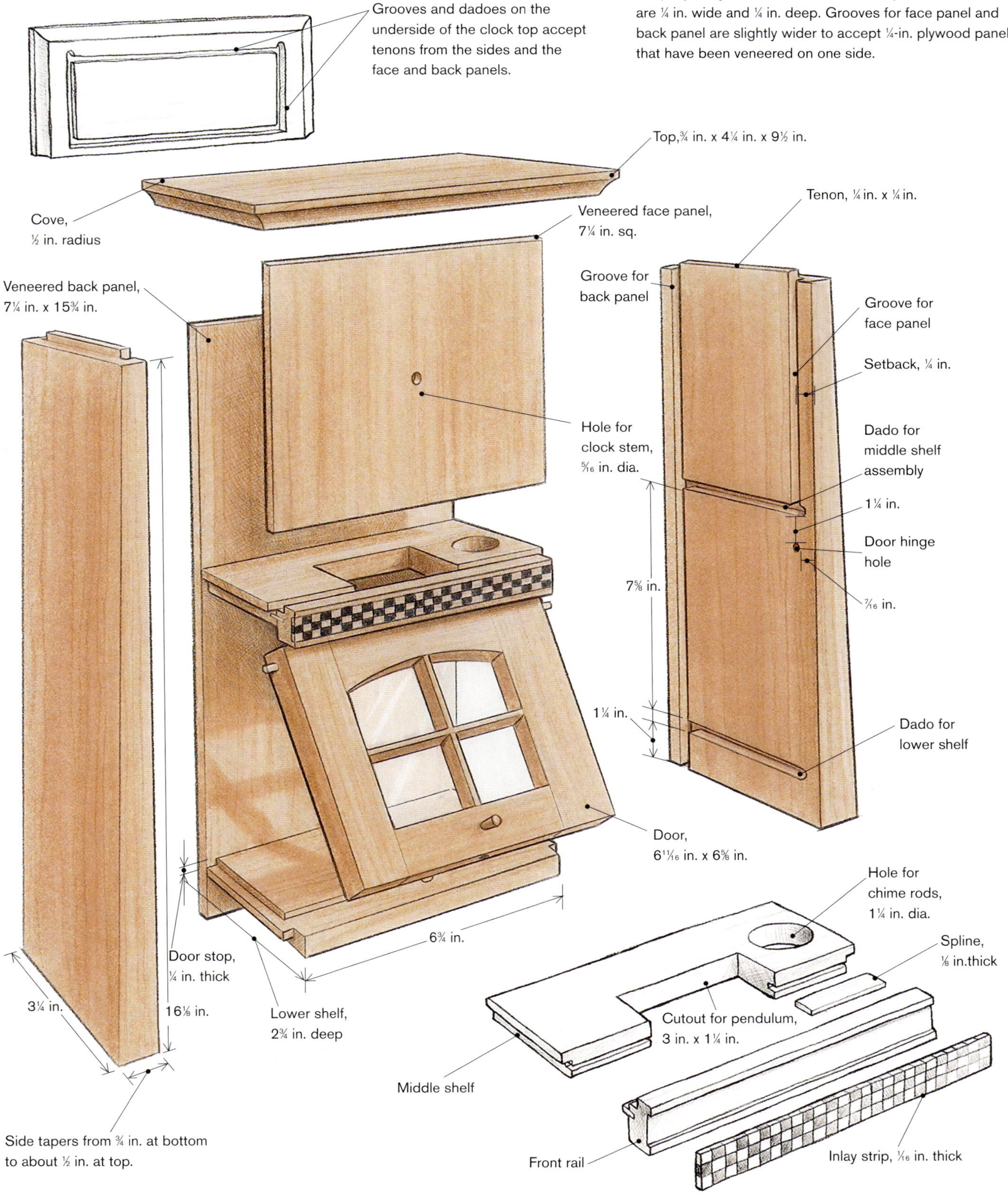

Cove, ½ in. radius

Top, ¾ in. x 4¼ in. x 9½ in.

Veneered face panel, 7¼ in. sq.

Tenon, ¼ in. x ¼ in.

Veneered back panel, 7¼ in. x 15¾ in.

Groove for back panel

Groove for face panel

Setback, ¼ in.

Hole for clock stem, ⁵⁄₁₆ in. dia.

Dado for middle shelf assembly

1¼ in.

7⅝ in.

Door hinge hole

⁷⁄₁₆ in.

1¼ in.

Dado for lower shelf

Door, 6¹¹⁄₁₆ in. x 6⅝ in.

Door stop, ¼ in. thick

6¾ in.

Hole for chime rods, 1¼ in. dia.

Spline, ⅛ in. thick

3¼ in.

16⅛ in.

Lower shelf, 2¾ in. deep

Cutout for pendulum, 3 in. x 1¼ in.

Middle shelf

Inlay strip, ¹⁄₁₆ in. thick

Side tapers from ¾ in. at bottom to about ½ in. at top.

Front rail

Making the Checkered Inlay

The checkerboard band across the middle of the clock is an eye-catching detail, and it really makes the clock. You'll find that it invites close inspection. For best results, use clean, straight material, and don't use any sapwood or wood with other defects. You'd only have to discard several strips of inlay later.

STEP 1

Prepare two "sandwiches" of material—one with a lighter wood in between two dark pieces, and the other just the opposite. Width and length aren't critical, but each layer of the laminations must be exactly ¼ in. thick.

STEP 2

Plane the edges of each lamination square to the faces and make sure the edges are free of glue. Crosscut laminations into segments exactly ¼ in. wide.

STEP 3

Arrange segments from alternating sandwiches. Glue and clamp them together. Apply pressure down, as well, onto a steel plate or something similar, to ensure even registration all the way across.

STEP 4

When the glue has cured, clean up and square the completed checkerboard blank. Bandsaw into 1⁄16-in.-thick strips. Using a knife to pull the thin strips along on the outfeed side of the blade helps. Select the best pieces for the clock inlay.

Making the Middle Shelf

PLANE THE FRONT RAIL FLUSH. Using a sharp block plane is a quick way to bring the top and bottom edges of the front rail down to the level of the inlay.

KERF FRONT RAIL AND MIDDLE SHELF FOR A SPLINE. One pass with each piece over a standard-width blade is plenty. Then just plane the spline to fit.

Use Router Table and Tablesaw for Joinery

The two sides of the clock are dadoed into the top, and the lower and middle shelves are dadoed to the sides. I routed these stopped dadoes as well as the grooves for the back panel and face panel on the router table. The dadoes are all ¼ in. deep by ¼ in. wide. I moved the router-table fence over a hair for the grooves, which are just slightly wider to accommodate the face and back panels. I made these from ¼-in. birch plywood, veneering one side with quartersawn pear veneer. To ensure accurate, square cuts on the router table, I used a right-angle jig

CHECK THE ALIGNMENT (left). The top of the middle shelf and the top of the front rail should be flush. The ¼-in. groove accepts the bottom edge of the face panel.

MIDDLE SHELF ASSEMBLY

The middle shelf assembly is 2¾ in. deep overall.

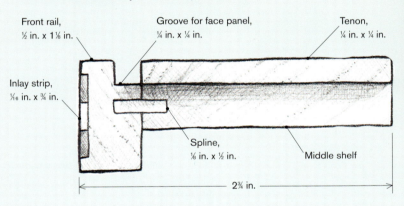

Front rail,
½ in. x 1⅛ in.

Groove for face panel,
¼ in. x ¼ in.

Tenon,
¼ in. x ¼ in.

Inlay strip,
⅛ in. x ¾ in.

Spline,
⅛ in. x ½ in.

Middle shelf

2¾ in.

MIDDLE SHELF AND FRONT RAIL ARE JOINED WITH A SPLINE. Hand screws provide plenty of clamping pressure, but be sure the front rail stays square to the shelf as pressure is applied.

and cut no more than ⅛ in. deep per pass. With the tablesaw, I cut the corresponding stub tenons at the top of the case sides and on the ends of the lower and middle shelves. They were cut just a little wide and then fitted by hand.

I tapered the outside faces of the clock sides using a jack plane, taking the sides from ¾ in. at the bottom to just under ½ in. at the top. This gives the clock a lighter feel and is a detail found on many Arts-and-Crafts clocks made earlier this century. A ½-in. cove routed around the underside of the clock's top gives it a visual lift.

With the top, bottom, and sides made and fitted, I planed and scraped the pieces. They were sprayed inside and out with two very thin coats of aerosol nitrocellulose sanding sealer followed by one coat of semigloss lacquer. To keep the joints free of lacquer, I taped the stub tenons and temporarily fit ¼-in. strips into all the dadoes. I scuff-sanded with 320-grit sandpaper between coats. Spraying before assembly allowed easy access into corners, eliminated drips, and reduced overspray.

Middle shelf–The middle shelf requires a 1¼-in.-dia. hole for chime rods and a 3-in. by 1¼-in. cutout for the pendulum. I made

A TEMPLATE AND GUIDE SHAPE THE TOP DOOR RAIL. After bandsawing the curve in the rail to rough shape, the author routs it to finished shape.

MUNTINS ARE TENONED INTO OPEN MORTISES IN FRAME. Tap the tenons home with a small hammer and a wooden block.

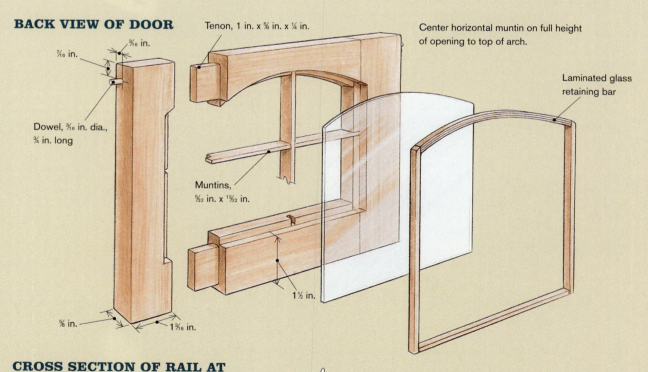

BACK VIEW OF DOOR

³⁄₁₆ in.

⁷⁄₁₆ in.

Dowel, ³⁄₁₆ in. dia., ¾ in. long

Tenon, 1 in. x ⅝ in. x ¼ in.

Center horizontal muntin on full height of opening to top of arch.

Laminated glass retaining bar

Muntins, ⁵⁄₃₂ in. x ¹³⁄₃₂ in.

1½ in.

⅝ in.

1³⁄₁₆ in.

CROSS SECTION OF RAIL AT MUNTIN INTERSECTION

Knob

Muntin tenon, ¼ in. x ⅛ in.

Tenon, ¼ in. dia.

⁷⁄₁₆ in.

½ in.

Bullet catch, top part, centered in bottom door rail

the hole on the drill press with a Forstner bit and cut out the cavity for the pendulum on the tablesaw and bandsaw.

A band of checkerboard inlay is let into a front rail, which is splined to the middle shelf. I used the tablesaw to cut the slot for the 1/8-in. spline and to cut the rabbet in the top of the front rail for the veneered face panel. To create the recess for the checkerboard inlay, I plowed a 1/16-in.-deep groove across the center of the front rail on the tablesaw and planed it smooth and flat. Then I glued and clamped down the checkerboard inlay, which I made of ebony and pear (see the sidebar on p. 66 for a complete description of making the inlay). After the glue had cured, I planed the front rail flush with the inlay (see the top right photo on p. 66), cut the front rail to length, and clamped up the middle shelf assembly (see the photo at right on p. 67). I taped the stub tenons and sprayed the assembly before moving on to the plywood panels for the clock face and back.

Veneer the Face and Back Panels

Because I didn't want to worry about wood movement across the width of the clock, I used 1/4-in.-thick birch plywood for the face and the back panels.

I veneered the plywood with clear, quartersawn pear. This way, the grain all but disappears. After shooting and taping the veneer seams, I glued the veneer to the plywood using yellow glue and a warm iron. Ordinarily, both sides of the substrate should be veneered so the piece won't cup later. But because both panels are captured, I didn't think it was necessary to veneer their inside faces.

After the glue had dried, I scraped the veneer tape off and cut the panels to size. To mark the center of the face for the clock movement, I struck diagonals from corner to corner and used an awl to make an impression where the lines crossed. Then I

scraped and sanded the pear veneer. I finished the face with sanding sealer and semigloss lacquer. By finishing the face before drilling for the clock stem, I didn't have to avoid the hole when I sanded or rubbed with steel wool.

I bored the hole for the clock movement on my drill press and screwed it to the back of the face panel (for part numbers, price, and other information on the movement, see Sources on p. 71). I set the back panel aside until the whole clock was glued up.

Glazed Door Swings Up on Dowel Hinges

The little door that swings up to provide access to the pendulum is of standard mortise-and-tenon construction. Both top and bottom rails are 1½ in. wide, slightly wider than the stiles. The top rail takes a mild curve, and the bottom accepts a small knob and visually anchors the design. I roughed out the curve in the top rail on the bandsaw, and then I cleaned it up using a template and the template guide on my router table (see the photo at left on p. 68).

After the door frame was glued up, I routed a 1/4-in. rabbet all around the inside to accept a pane of glass. I squared the corners of the rabbet and chopped small open-sided mortises in the back side of the door for the muntin assembly (see the photo at right on p. 68).

I ripped the muntin stock on the tablesaw and planed and scraped it to its final 5/32 in. thickness. I cut the tenons on the ends of the muntins with a small dovetail saw and fitted them to the mortises in the back of the door with a file. The half-lap joint where the two muntins cross was done on the tablesaw. After gluing in the muntin assembly and letting it dry, I planed it flush with the front of the door frame.

I cut the glass for the door, but the edges were still a bit ragged, so I cleaned them up on a belt sander clamped into my

A coarsely grained or heavily figured wood could overpower a clock of this size.

ASSEMBLE THE CLOCK ON ITS SIDE, turn it upright, and then place the top on the clock. Adjust the clamps as necessary to make the case square.

not difficult. Before drilling the holes in the sides of the door, I did a test with a piece of scrap the same size as my door. I wanted to be sure the door wouldn't bind on the bottom edge of the front rail when opened and that it would set back ¼ in. into the clock case.

To drill the hinge holes in the door, I used a doweling jig and a handheld drill. I drilled the holes in the case sides on the drill press, shimming the underside of the thinner end to get the sides level.

The dowel I used was a little too fat to fit in the holes I had drilled, so I shaved it with a block plane before cutting it to length—about ¾ in. to start.

I dry-fitted the door in the clock case and fine-tuned the length of the dowels with a file until I had an even reveal on both sides of the case, without much play.

Door knob is turned from a blank shaped to a Morse taper–The small pull is made of the same wood as the clock case. I first shaped a 1-in.-sq., 3-in.-long piece of pear into a rough Morse taper, leaving about ¾ in. at the end for the knob. I cut off the end the drive spurs had bitten into, replaced the drive center with the tapered plug, and tapped it securely in place. With the end free, but secure, I turned a small knob. Then I sanded, burnished, and finished it right on the lathe before cutting it free from the tapered plug with a small tenon saw.

I marked the location of the knob mortise at the center of the bottom door rail and drilled it on the drill press. After some final fitting of the knob tenon with a file and sandpaper, I glued and clamped the knob to the door using a handscrew.

To hold the door in place when it's closed, I used a ¼-in. bullet catch made by Brusso and sold through many woodworking-supply catalogs. The Brusso catch is the cleanest, smallest, and least intrusive one I've seen.

bench vise. A 100-grit belt eased the edges quickly but safely.

To hold the glass in the rabbet in the back of the door frame, I spot-glued a laminated, curved bar across the top and straight strips against the two sides and the bottom. I made the curved bar from three thin strips, using the top rail as a form and planing them flush after the glue had dried. Because these retaining bars are just glued to the frame in a few spots each, they can be pried out and the glass replaced, if necessary. When the glue had dried, I scraped, sanded, and finished the door.

Location of dowel hinge holes is critical–I wanted the door on this clock to swing up rather than out, and I didn't want to mar the clock's appearance with metal hardware. My solution was to pivot the door on two short sections of ³⁄₁₆-in.-dia. dowel set into holes in the door's edge and on the inside of the clock case. The exact placement of the holes is critical, but it's

I dry-assembled the clock, with the door in place. The door is positioned correctly when it is set back from the front edge of the case by ¼ in. evenly top to bottom. I marked straight down from the front edge of the door at its center. Then I located the center of the bottom part of the bullet catch ⁵⁄₁₆ in. back from that mark. I centered the top part of the catch on the ⅜-in.-thick door. The hole in the door can be bored freehand. But I drilled the hole in the bottom shelf on a drill press. Both pieces of the bullet catch can be pushed in place. No glue is needed.

Assemble Case on Its Side

I laid one side of the case on the workbench and glued in the bottom and middle shelves. Next, I slid in the veneered face panel with the works attached. I set in the completed door and then carefully lowered the other case side, lining up all the mating parts. After standing the clock upright, I glued the top on and clamped up the whole assembly, side to side and top to bottom. I adjusted the clamps until the case was square (see the photo on the facing page). The back of the clock, which slides home in a groove, goes on last.

After the glue had dried, I cut, planed, and finished one side of a ¼-in.-thick door stop. I glued the door stop onto the bottom shelf, using spring clamps to hold it in place until the glue had set. The bullet catch provides a positive stop for the door, but the door stop will prevent the door from being inadvertently jammed past the catch, possibly breaking the hinge dowels or the case itself.

Snap Pendulum Rod to Size and Attach Hands

The pendulum hanger extends down into the lower compartment through the cutout in the middle shelf. The hanger supports the adjustable pendulum shaft. The pendulum shaft is manufactured with scored lines across its back so that it can be broken to length. I broke off the shaft so the center of the pendulum bob would swing past the crosshairs formed by the muntins of the door.

I positioned the one-piece dial and bezel over the clock stem extending through the veneered face panel (the dial is the face of the clock; the bezel is the brass-bound glass disc). Then I fastened the dial with a thin brass nut. I press-fitted the hands over the stem and screwed on the top nut. Each hand has a slot or hole that corresponds with a portion of the dial stem. Next, I tacked the dial in place with the eight tiny brads that came with it. Once the dial was tacked down, I put in a D battery and turned on the clock.

Finally, I turned the clock upside down (after temporarily removing the pendulum shaft and bob) and slid the back of the case in from the bottom. I secured it with two ¾-in. #8 brass screws driven into the back edge of the bottom shelf. The removable back makes it easy to change the battery or turn off the clock.

MARIO RODRIGUEZ teaches woodworking at the Fashion Institute of Technology in New York City. He is a contributing editor to *Fine Woodworking* magazine.

Sources

The quartz Bim-Bam movement and the dial-bezel combination are from

Merritt's Antiques
P.O. Box 277
Douglassville, PA
19518-0277
800-345-4101
The movement is part
#P-647W/P and costs
$41. The dial-bezel combination is part #P-222
and costs $19.

The hands are from
S. LaRose
3223 Yanceyville St.
P.O. Box 21208
Greensboro, NC 27420
910-621-1936
The hands are part
#816012 and cost 75¢.

Building a Shaker Wall Clock

BY CHRIS BECKSVOORT

Isaac Newton Youngs, a Shaker brother who lived in the Sabbathday Lake community in New Gloucester, Maine, built only 14 of these clocks, yet they still stand out as a hallmark of Shaker style. Some clocks were built with a glass door below, and a few were made with glass set into the side panels. My favorite is still housed at Sabbathday Lake and looks closer to the one I build. But you couldn't say that mine is an exact reproduction of the 1840 versions. Furniture reproduction is a slippery phrase. Though I'm known as a Shaker furniture maker, only twice in my career have I been asked to build historically accurate Shaker reproductions, meaning that all wood, hardware, dimensions, joinery techniques, tooling, and finishes must match the original.

I have no qualms with historical accuracy, except when it comes to techniques that may have worked in the past but are not suitable to-day. Wood movement is one of those areas. The Shakers did not have to deal with forced hot-air heat. We do. Shaker clock makers built their cases to fit their mechanisms. We must build our cases to fit mechanisms that are commercially available today. To me, that seems perfectly aligned with Shaker ideals.

For starters, the original clock was constructed predominantly of white pine. I chose cherry for its color, hardness, and grain. Because cherry moves more than white pine does, I had to make a few dimensional adjustments to allow for wood movement of the back panel. Second, I decided to use a top-of-the-line mechanical movement, which required a small amount of additional interior space. Consequently, my overall case is a little deeper, and the back is a bit thinner. So much for historical accuracy.

The construction of both the original and my version is as simple as the spare design. I will offer several options—in construction techniques, dimensional changes, and

Build the Case

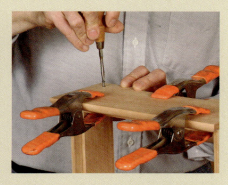

LONG-GRAIN PLUGS ARE HARDLY SEEN. The top is screwed straight into the sides, then plugged and trimmed flush.

ALLOW THE BACK TO MOVE. The back is screwed only near the center. The edges are then nailed into place, allowing for seasonal movement.

QUICK CLAMPS FOR TEMPORARY STRENGTH. The false top and false bottom are simply butt-joined and glued to the sides. The actual top and bottom will reinforce this joint. Before the glue sets, check to make sure the case is level and square.

types of mechanisms—to suit the type of clock you want to build. Accurate dimensions for the original clocks (the glass-door, not the panel-door version) can be found in John Kassay's *The Book of Shaker Furniture* (University of Massachusetts Press, 1980) or (for the clock with glass panels in the sides) in Enjer Handberg's *Shaker Furniture and Woodenware* (Berkshire Traveller Press, 1991). The version I built appears in my book, *The Shaker Legacy* (The Taunton Press, 1998).

Make the Case to Fit the Clock Parts

I never start construction on a clock until I have the movement, dial, and hands. Having these at the ready makes it much easier to fit the dial and allow proper clearance between the shaft, the hands, and the glass, as well as the clock movement and the case back. I hate surprises.

Once you have the clock parts, you can cut the sides of the case to size. Then cut ⅜-in. by ½-in. rabbets to accept the back. The front of each side receives a stopped rabbet to accept the face. You could simply make the clock an inch wider and avoid cutting rabbets in the front, but—for reasons more aesthetic than historical— I prefer to keep proportions closer to the original.

Next, cut the top and bottom pieces and mold them with a quarter-round

A SHAKER WALL CLOCK

This adaptation of an 1840 Shaker clock features simple case construction and straightforward door joinery. A hand-painted face is a handsome touch, and a quality movement will keep the clock running smoothly for years to come.

Quarter-round moldings, ³⁄₁₆ in. x ³⁄₁₆ in.

Rails and stiles, ½ in. thick x 1 in. wide

Glass supports, ¼ in. x ¼ in.

Upper door, 10 in. wide x 10 in. tall

Panel, ³⁄₁₆ in. thick

Lower door, 10 in. wide x 19⅞ in. tall

Rails and stiles, ½ in. thick x 1⅜ in. wide

Notch, ½ in. x 4½ in., accepts the hanger.

Top, ⅝ in. thick x 4½ in. wide x 11 in. long, is shaped with a roundover bit.

Hanger, 4½ in. dia.

Hanger hole, 1⅛ in. dia.

Back, ½ in. thick x 9½ in. wide x 34⅞ in. long, is glued and screwed at the center.

False top, ½ in. thick x 3 in. wide x 9 in. long

Stopped rabbet, ¼ in. x ¼ in. x 11 in.

Filler strips, ½ in. thick x 1½ in. wide x 10½ in. long, support the clock face.

Divider, ⅝ in. thick x 1⅛ in. wide x 9½ in. long

Bullnose molding, ¾ in. thick x ½ in. wide x 10 in. long

Rabbet, ⅜ in. x ½ in., accepts the back.

Bottom, ⅝ in. thick x 4½ in. wide x 11 in. long, is shaped with a roundover bit.

Case sides, ½ in. thick x 3½ in. wide x 30⅜ in. long

router bit. The back of the top is notched out ½ in. by 4½ in. to allow for the hanger on the back of the case.

On the original, the top and bottom were merely nailed onto the sides. I use long, thin screws and plugs. Another alternative is dowels. I once had a student who attempted to use sliding dovetails, only to discover that they lasted from 12:00 until noon. With only ³⁄₁₆ in. of overhang on the

sides and part of that cut away by the rabbet, the remaining end grain is extremely fragile.

I prefer to use a false bottom and top, which not only make glue-up easier but also act as a doorstop in front and create rabbets to house the back. Glue the false top and bottom to the sides using butt joints. Once the glue dries, center the actual top and bottom on the case and screw them into the sides.

The clock back simply butts up against the false top and bottom and is screwed into place from behind. However, this is where wood movement comes into play. The back is about 9½ in. wide, which means that a piece of flatsawn cherry will move about ³⁄₃₂ in. (from 6 percent moisture content in winter to 13 percent moisture content in summer). If you can locate or glue up a quartersawn back, the amount of movement is cut in half, to ³⁄₆₄ in. So, if you're building in the summer, when the back has reached a moisture content of near 12 percent or 13 percent, the back can be fitted tightly. In the winter, when the moisture content of the back is closer to 6 percent, a gap of just under ³⁄₆₄ in. is required on each side. Also, leave a small gap where the half-round hanger protrudes through the top.

Another change I make is to increase the size of the hanger hole, from ½ in. to 1⅛ in., to allow the clock to be hung on a Shaker peg. The back is merely nailed into place, with a dab of glue in the center to ensure that wood movement is equal in both directions.

Next, let in the two-piece molded divider between the top and bottom doors. A horizontal divider, which also acts as a doorstop, is set into the rabbet flush with the face, and then a bullnose molding is glued over it.

At this point it pays to plan ahead. Measure the depth of the movement to check that you have proper clearance for both the shaft and the glass of the door. Mechanical movements are either attached directly to the back—as I've done—or sit on a shelf. Quartz movements, being much shallower, are usually attached to the dial. If you use a spacer, the movement can also be attached to the case back. Planning ahead allows you to position the dial so that the hand shaft is close to the glass but does not touch it.

DOOR-JOINERY DETAILS

UPPER DOOR

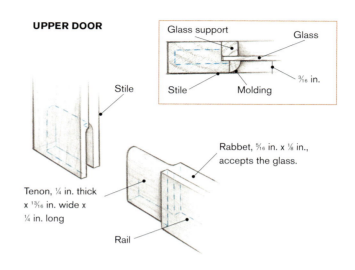

Stile

Glass support

Glass

Stile

Molding

³⁄₁₆ in.

Tenon, ¼ in. thick x ¹³⁄₁₆ in. wide x ¼ in. long

Rabbet, ⁵⁄₁₆ in. x ⅛ in., accepts the glass.

Rail

LOWER DOOR

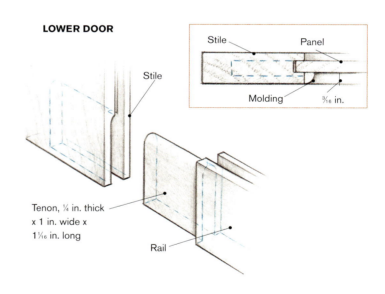

Stile

Panel

Molding

³⁄₁₆ in.

Stile

Tenon, ¼ in. thick x 1 in. wide x 1¹⁄₁₆ in. long

Rail

Once you've established the location of the dial, glue two vertical filler strips to the inside of the case. Thick metal dials like the one I used can be screwed to these strips directly, while thin metal or paper dials should be adhered to ¼-in.-thick plywood backings.

Simple joinery for the doors

The doors are relatively straightforward, mortised and tenoned at each corner. Cut

Fit the Door Divider

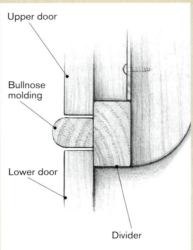

HORIZONTAL DIVIDER CATCHES THE DOORS. The horizontal divider is sized to act as a doorstop for both doors. It is set into the stopped rabbet that holds the clock face.

Upper door

Bullnose molding

Lower door

Divider

BULLNOSE MOLDING SEPARATES TOP AND BOTTOM DOORS. Shape the profile using a roundover bit, then cut it to fit flush with the sides.

haunched mortise-and-tenon joints on center, and make sure to offset the glass and panel grooves to allow room for the thumbnail profile along the fronts. The frames are ½ in. thick, and the bottom panel is only 3⁄16 in. thick. The 3⁄16-in. quarter-round moldings are added after the panel is in place. On the top door, add the quarter-round moldings to hold the glass on the outside, and add 3⁄16-in. glass supports, nailed from the inside, to hold the back of the glass.

From looking at the original, I can't tell how the doors are kept closed. Nor does Kassay give any clue. When in doubt, I take historical liberties, using something that is period appropriate and might have been used. I usually turn my knobs with extended shafts and attach a small oval spinner. I chisel out a small mortise for the spinner on the inside of

both the upper and lower cases. This method is unobtrusive, and it works.

As far as I know, nobody makes hands to match the originals. When in doubt, select the simplest design possible, such as moon or spade hands. If you are handy with sheet metal, you can cut your own. If you decide to get the expensive mechanical movement, you can have custom hands made to specifications.

As far as a finish goes, I am partial to Tried & True Varnish Oil. It leaves a silky, penetrating finish that I prefer. More accurate for this clock would be a shellac finish, which was used on the original.

When hanging the clock from a peg board, carve a ½-in. flat spot at the top of the peg where it meets the hanger, leaving a slight ridge, to keep the clock from sliding forward on the peg. If the peg board is ¾ in.

Construct the Doors

DON'T RISK SURPRISES. Before applying glue, carefully dry-fit the doors and see that they fit the case.

QUARTER-ROUND MOLDING TRIMS OUT THE DOOR. The molding is shaped on the router, then mitered to fit the door. Becksvoort simply glues the molding to the rails and the stiles.

SECURING THE GLASS. After setting the glass into the rabbet, small glass supports are nailed into place.

thick, use a ¾-in. spacer behind and near the bottom of the clock. A toggle bolt or similar anchor will attach the spacer to drywall or plaster if there is no stud nearby. Once the clock is perfectly plumb and running smoothly, drill a hole through the back into the spacer and anchor the clock with a screw. This keeps it from shifting during winding or an accidental bump.

CHRIS BECKSVOORT makes Shaker-style furniture in Maine and is a contributing editor to *Fine Wood-working* magazine.

A Movement for Every Price Range

By far the least expensive movement is the battery-powered quartz movement. It is also the most accurate and the least fussy and bothersome. Change the battery once a year, and that's it. These movements are also the smallest and easiest to mount. The cost is anywhere from $5 to $30, and you can get a pendulum to boot. Sounds perfect, doesn't it?

The fact is, I can spot their fake pendulums a mile away. They have a weird little groan and oscillate too slowly. Still, if money is a concern, they're worth considering. Quartz movements are available in craft catalogs and also from Woodcraft Supply (800-225-1153; www.woodcraft.com), Murray Clock Craft (800-268-3181; www.murrayclock.com) and Merritt's Clock Supply (800-345-4101; www.merritts.com).

In my opinion, mechanical movements are much more in keeping with period clocks. Most require a little extra work to install and to get the pendulum adjusted to the correct time. Plus, they need to be wound every week. Most are face-mounted, which requires the face to be backed by ¼-in.-thick plywood. The lower-end mechanical movements run from about $35.

The price for a spring-driven, time-only (silent) movement is about $40 ($110 for a unit with a 20-in. pendulum). You can also spend more and get chimes or a bell strike. The downside to these movements is that they have a life expectancy of roughly five years if oiled yearly. The brass plates are thin and soft and, after a few years of use, will wear out. They can be repaired but will require the services of a clock maker to install bushings.

ALIGN THE MOVEMENT WITH THE FACE. With the movement roughly centered inside the clock, lay the face in place and make adjustments until the hands are properly centered. Use an awl to make screw holes through the movement.

Inexpensive mechanical movements can be ordered from the same suppliers listed previously.

I am quite fussy, and I would not expect my customers to purchase a high-priced clock that took 40 hours to make, only to have to replace bushings after two years. A quality case demands a quality movement. I wanted a time-only, weight-driven movement made of thick, hardened brass plates. To me, this high-quality movement comes closest to what the original Shaker movements must have been like. I don't mind the extra time it takes to install the movement or the extra time required to adjust the pendulum to get it to keep perfect time. The weekly winding with the crank key becomes a Sunday night ritual.

The banjo movement is available from Merritt's Clock Supply with weight, pendulum, and winder for $225. Individually made wall-clock movements are available for $300. Add another $50 for custom-cut hands and $25 for unpainted, heavy steel dial blanks direct from David Lindow, clock maker (527 Gravity Road, Lake Ariel, PA 18436; 570-937-3301).

Custom dials and dial painting are available from The Dial House (3971 Buchanan Hwy., Dallas, GA 30132; 770-943-5370).

Build a Wall Shelf

BY PETER TURNER

My wife, Colleen, occasionally asks me to build a piece of furniture for our home. I would love nothing more than to honor these requests, but there never seems to be time. But a hanging shelf is one project that I figured I could finish quickly.

I got the inspiration from a drawing of a peg-hung Shaker shelf in Ejner Handberg's book *Shop Drawings of Shaker Furniture and Woodenware, Vol II* (Berkshire Traveller Press, 1975). The shelf sides in Handberg's drawing are curved on top, but the bottom is straight. I added another curve at the bottom, experimenting with different curves until one satisfied my eye. Handberg's Shaker shelves also hung from a wall-mounted peg rail. I don't have a peg rail at home, so the first time I made this piece, I used brass keyhole hangers. In later versions, including the one shown on right, I used simpler brass hangers mortised into the second shelf from the top. These are less expensive, are easier to install, and make

SHAKE UP YOUR WALL WITH A SHELF. This simple wall-hung shelf, perfect for a spice rack or seashells, was adapted from a traditional Shaker design. The shelves are joined to the sides with sliding dovetails.

Wall Shelf
Step-by-Step

STEP 1

ROUTING DOVETAIL GROOVES IN THE SIDES.

After milling all the material to a thickness of ½ in., cut the sides to length, but leave them at least ¼ in. wider than the widest dimension (4⅜ in.). Then mark the centerlines for each shelf on both pieces. Using a slotted piece of plywood to guide a ½-in. router template insert, cut the dovetail slots. First rough the slots with a ¼-in. straight bit, then finish them off with a ⅜-in. dovetail bit.

STEP 2

TRACE THE PATTERN AND BANDSAW THE SIDES.
With the grooves routed, cut the curved and tapered sides. First make a plywood pattern matching the shape of the sides of the shelf, trace the pattern onto the back of each side, and bandsaw the shape close to the line.

STEP 3

FLUSH-TRIMMING BIT MAKES BOTH SIDES IDENTICAL. After roughing out the sides on the bandsaw or jigsaw, clamp each side into the plywood pattern using hold-down clamps fastened to the plywood. Then rout the edge with a ½-in. flush-trimming bit, either using a router table (see the drawing on p. 82) or a hand-held router setup. This step will remove any tearout created when you routed the dovetail grooves, and it makes each side identical.

STEP 4

ROUTING THE DOVETAILS ON THE SHELVES. To cut the dovetails, mount your router horizontally on the router table (see the drawing on p. 82). This makes it easier to adjust the height of the cut. It also lets you hold the workpiece flat on the table rather than against a fence. Adjust the depth and height of the router bit to match the depth of the slots. I cut the tails to fit by trial and error, testing on scrap stock milled at the same time as the shelf parts.

STEP 5

CUT SHELVES TO WIDTH AND ASSEMBLE. Don't cut the shelves to width until after you cut the dovetails on the ends, so you can remove any tearout caused by the router. The front edge of the top three shelves is angled to match the tapered sides, which you can do by transferring the angle to the jointer fence. After sanding all the pieces, slide each shelf into the sides, starting at the bottom and clamping each shelf as you go.

SHAKER SHELF UPDATED

Traditional, peg-hung Shaker wall shelves often have a slight curve at the top and taper from top to bottom. This shelf has a curve at the bottom also, and only the top half is tapered. The piece can be modified by changing the width or the shelf arrangement.

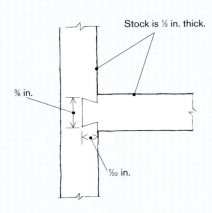

Stock is ½ in. thick.

⅜ in.

⁷⁄₃₂ in.

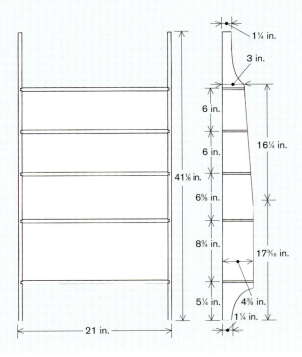

21 in.

1¼ in.

3 in.

6 in.

6 in.

41⅛ in.

6⅝ in.

8¾ in.

5¼ in.

16¼ in.

17³⁄₁₆ in.

4⅜ in.

1¼ in.

HORIZONTAL DOVETAILING FIXTURE MAKES A DIFFICULT JOINT EASY

Cutting sliding dovetails can be tricky. To get a long tail to slide snugly into its groove requires a uniform cut. Rather than holding the shelves vertically to cut the dovetails, you can mount the router horizontally on a standard router table, as shown. Holding the workpiece flat on the table, cut one side of the tail; then turn the piece over and cut the other side. Use scrap of the same thickness to establish the exact height and depth of the dovetail bit, and then fit them in a test groove to prevent marring the final pieces.

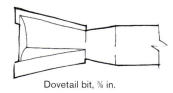

Dovetail bit, ⅜ in.

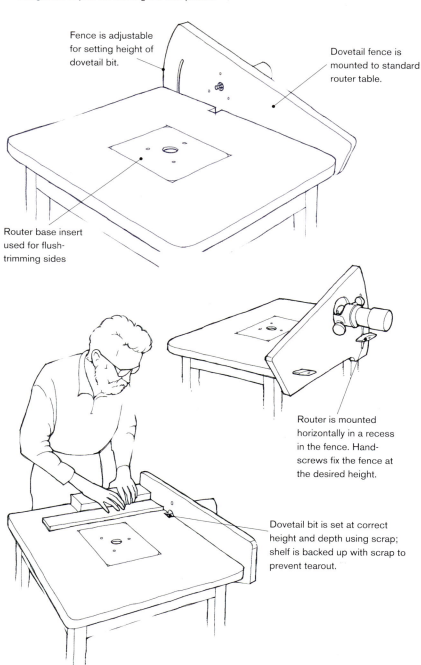

Fence is adjustable for setting height of dovetail bit.

Dovetail fence is mounted to standard router table.

Router base insert used for flush-trimming sides

Router is mounted horizontally in a recess in the fence. Hand-screws fix the fence at the desired height.

Dovetail bit is set at correct height and depth using scrap; shelf is backed up with scrap to prevent tearout.

hanging the shelf a snap. We use one hanging shelf as a spice rack. The varying heights and sizes of our spice jars helped establish the shelf spacing and overall width.

Consistency is the key to this piece. If you start with flat stock of uniform thickness and length, the joinery follows smoothly. To ensure consistency, do all your milling at once (all the stock is ½ in. thick) and use a plywood pattern and flush-trimming router bit for making identical curved and tapered sides.

The trickiest parts of this piece are the sliding dovetails. Routing the grooves is easy, but the long tails on the ends of each shelf take some patience and finesse. I use a router setup in which the router is mounted horizontally; it seems to make it easier to get a straight, even cut (see the drawing at left).

By holding the pieces flat on the router table, I have more control as I slide the piece past the bit. I make test pieces out of scrap, which I milled at the same time as the final pieces.

The Shakers housed the shelves in dadoes, rather than sliding dovetails, and you can do the same. It won't be as strong, but if you're worried about the shelves, you can toenail them from the bottom with finish nails or brads.

PETER TURNER is a woodworker and furniture maker who lives in Portland, Maine.

Colonial Cupboard

This little cabinet is based on a late-18th-century original owned by a friend of mine. It's a rare piece, and antique dealers regularly pester him about selling it. The dealers want his cabinet for the same reason you will want to make it. There is always demand for an attractive and handy storage space.

The cabinet is interesting for woodworkers for two reasons: First, it's a tutorial on hand-cut joinery. Although a small piece, this cabinet requires nine types of joints. You will get some practice on dovetails, dadoes, rabbets, shiplaps, coping, miters, panel-in-groove, and mortises and tenons (both blind and through). While

BY MIKE DUNBAR

Freestanding cabinet offers a tutorial on hand-cut joinery.

A DOVETAILED BOX IS THE FOUNDATION

Shelves, back boards, face frame, cornice, and bracket base all attach to the dovetailed case. Then, all that's left is the frame-and-panel door.

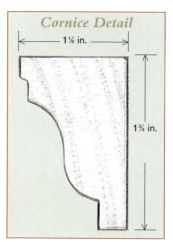

Cornice Detail

1⅛ in.

1¾ in.

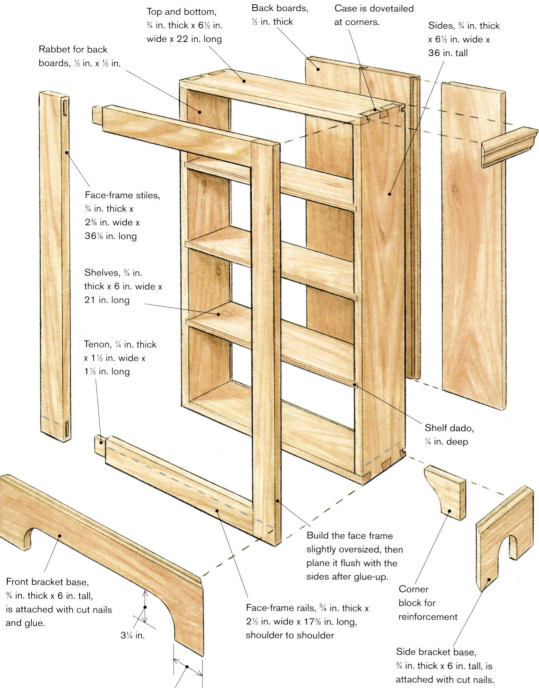

Rabbet for back boards, ½ in. x ½ in.

Top and bottom, ¾ in. thick x 6½ in. wide x 22 in. long

Back boards, ½ in. thick

Case is dovetailed at corners.

Sides, ¾ in. thick x 6½ in. wide x 36 in. tall

Face-frame stiles, ¾ in. thick x 2⅜ in. wide x 36⅛ in. long

Shelves, ¾ in. thick x 6 in. wide x 21 in. long

Tenon, ¼ in. thick x 1½ in. wide x 1½ in. long

Shelf dado, ¼ in. deep

Front bracket base, ¾ in. thick x 6 in. tall, is attached with cut nails and glue.

3¼ in.

2½ in.

Build the face frame slightly oversized, then plane it flush with the sides after glue-up.

Face-frame rails, ¾ in. thick x 2½ in. wide x 17⅜ in. long, shoulder to shoulder

Corner block for reinforcement

Side bracket base, ¾ in. thick x 6 in. tall, is attached with cut nails.

Shelf Detail

3/16 in.

¾ in.

BEAD THE FRONT EDGES OF THE SHELVES. The author uses a flat-head screw driven into a dowel to cut a small groove in each edge.

Bracket-Base Detail

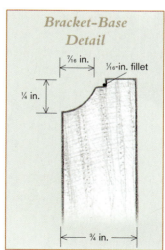

7/16 in.

1/16-in. fillet

¼ in.

¾ in.

Quick Dadoes with a Utility Knife and Chisel

MATCHING DADOES. Butt the sides against each other and lay out the locations of shelf dadoes (1). Use a utility knife to scribe the edges as deeply as possible (2), then pare out the waste with a chisel (3). Scribe and pare until you reach final depth. If you have one, use a router plane to clean up the bottom of the dado.

some of the work would be more straightforward if it were done on machines, there is value in sharpening your hand-tool skills (and certainly less dust and noise). The choice is yours, of course.

Second, this cabinet is a chameleon. It can be expressed in a host of ways. It's a good example of how a piece of furniture can be dressed up or down (see the examples on p. 88).

Another plus is that you can drastically change this cabinet's dimensions to make it fit a particular space or application: My cabinet was designed to house my eight-year-old's videocassette collection. You can even substitute a base molding for the bracket base and hang this cupboard on a wall.

Most of the stock is either ¾-in.-thick or ½-in.-thick pine. The cornice is 5/4 stock. I went to a local home center and bought #2 common boards, 1x8x12. There are so many small parts to the cupboard that I was able to work around most of the large knots or place them in shelves or back boards. The dime-sized knots that appear in the carcase and door gave me just the look I had wanted—not too perfect but not knotty pine, either.

As you build the piece, remember to use reference marks to keep track of parts and their positions.

The Carcase Comes First

There are two large dovetails on each corner. Although it makes no real difference,

Nail on the Face Frame and Back

ATTACH THE FACE FRAME WITH GLUE AND 4D CUT NAILS. These fasteners are appropriate to the period, and their thin, rectangular heads—aligned with the grain—are less obtrusive than round ones.

SHIPLAPPED BACK BOARDS. The boards are rabbeted with the fillister to create the shiplap joints. When nailing on the boards, leave gaps between them to allow for seasonal movement.

my habit is to lay out the pins first. I sized the pins by eye, so each joint varies slightly. Because the dovetails are mostly covered by the cornice or the bracket base, uniformity does not matter.

Dry-assemble the dovetails to test their fit. Also, check the case for square by measuring the diagonals from one corner to the opposite corner. If the measurements are the same, the case is square.

Rabbets and dadoes–Once the carcase has been dovetailed, rabbet the back to accept the back boards. Cut the rabbets with an adjustable rabbet plane (called a fillister), and clean them up with a shoulder plane. For a neater joint, check your progress with a small square. The four rabbets will leave small, square openings where they meet on the carcase, but these are visible only from the back.

Arrange the shelf placement to accommodate your cabinet's intended purpose. Lay out the dadoes on one side. Instead of measuring for the dadoes on the other side, match up the sides so their inside faces are touching. Then transfer the layout marks from one side to the other. Direct layout techniques are always preferable to trusting a tape measure and your memory.

In the past, every woodworker owned a dado plane. But no one makes them anymore, and the originals are expensive. You can use a multiplane like a Stanley No. 45 if you have one, but I find these all-in-one molding planes very difficult to use. You can make these dadoes with nothing more complicated than a utility knife and a chisel. Score straight lines along each edge of the dado and pare out the waste between them. Score and pare until you are at the desired depth. You can speed things up by using a router plane (also called a widow's tooth) to regulate the depth of the dado.

Once the carcase is finished, glue it up and clamp it, measuring diagonals to check for square.

The Face Frame

The door is hung inside a face frame joined with blind mortises and tenons. You don't want to risk this frame being slightly smaller than the cabinet, so leave the stiles and rails a little wide: About ⅛ in. per side is enough. After the face frame has been applied, you can handplane its edges flush with the carcase. Also, leave the stiles 4 in. longer than necessary. This will result in "horns" on both ends that can be trimmed when you are fitting the face frame to the carcase. These horns make it less likely that you will split the mortises or break out their tops while chopping them.

Before laying out the joints, mark the front and outside edges as reference surfaces and number the corners. Use a marking or mortise gauge to lay out the mortises and tenons. For accuracy, use a single edge as a reference surface for the gauge's fence. Chop the mortises with a mortise chisel and cut the tenons with a backsaw. Fit each joint and then test-fit the entire frame. Check for square. If you are satisfied, glue and clamp it. Afterward, trim the horns with a backsaw.

In keeping with the period, I glued and nailed the face fame to the cabinet with 4d cut nails, leaving the heads flush with the surface. The rectangular heads of cut nails are attractive and also less obvious than round heads. I purchase my cut nails from the Tremont Nail Co.

Finally, plane the face frame flush with the carcase.

Shelves and Back Boards

The shelf fronts are molded, and if you wish to include this feature, choose stock that is knot-free along one edge. The molding profile—called an astragal—is a traditional way of decorating shelves. If you don't have a way of making this shape, you can run a small bead on each edge with a simple scratch stock.

Cut the shelves to length and fit them into their dadoes. There is no need to secure them with fasteners or glue because they will be held captive by the back boards and face frame.

The back boards are shiplapped, meaning the boards have two rabbets that overlap. Shiplapped boards allow for seasonal movement without gaps opening. Quick word of caution: If you are making this cabinet in the summer, you can fit the back boards tightly together; however, if you make the piece during the heating season, fit the back boards loosely, giving them room to expand.

The Cornice

You have two considerations when choosing a profile for the crown molding. The most important is that the cornice be in scale with the cabinet. The type of profile is less important; it depends on how accurate you wish to be to a particular period. The ogee is typical of the 18th century, but other shapes came into vogue during the 1790s and early 1800s.

I used an appropriately sized ogee molding plane to make the cornice. This would be a great time to tune up that antique molding plane you own and learn to use it.

When you run moldings by hand, it is important to use straight-grained stock. Also, it's much easier to mold a single piece of wood long enough for the front and two sides at once.

This cabinet is a chameleon. It's a good example of how a piece can be dressed up or down.

DETAILS MAKE THE DIFFERENCE

As built, this cabinet contains a fairly standard 18th-century vocabulary. By changing a few of these elements, you can shift the pedigree and overall appearance of the piece.

MOLD THE CORNICE WITH AN OGEE MOLDING PLANE. Take all three pieces of the cornice from the same stock. Cut the stock wider than necessary to handle the cutting pressure.

Dentil molding

Make the cabinet more formal by building it of walnut or mahogany and adding complexity, including a dentil molding, to the cornice.

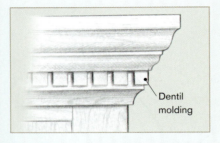

Bring the cabinet into the early 1800s by using a Federal-style molding for the cornice and a flat door panel with either an ovolo or an ogee on the stiles and rails. If you do so, use butt hinges and a later-style catch.

Molding plane

Workpiece

Spring lines

Many molding planes are designed to be tilted in use. Spring lines offer the user a visual reference for maintaining the proper angle while planing.

Finally, create a country look by trading the moldings for simple bevels.

FIT THE MITERS TO EACH OTHER. Cut the front piece to size and tack it on temporarily. Then trim the miters on each side piece to fit the front piece. A good way to do this is to hold a block plane against your chest and drag the miter across it.

Today, we usually cut miters with a tablesaw or a miter saw. The hand method is to use a miter box and backsaw. The miter box is simple to make. But be careful not to cut the miters going the wrong way. Draw an angled line showing which way each cut has to go.

If you need to trim a miter to fit, a low-angle block plane is ideal. Hold the tool against your chest and pull the miter over the cutting edge. This method lets you cut precisely and only where you want to.

The cornice is also nailed to the cabinet with cut nails. Add glue between the mitered ends of the molding to stop them from opening up later. The top of the cabinet is visible, so use a handplane to level off the cornice and dovetails.

Bracket Base

The upper edge of the bracket base is molded with a stepped cove. Furniture makers borrowed the cove from 18th-century architecture, but they added a small step at the top, called a fillet, to create another shadow line.

After cutting and testing the miters, make the scroll cuts along the bottom of each piece. I use either a small bowsaw or a coping saw. Here's a tip: It is easier to control a coping saw if you set it up to cut on the pull stroke.

Attach the base to the cabinet with cut nails. Then flip over the cabinet and glue in corner blocks, which will help strengthen the base.

Raised-Panel Door

The raised-panel door is your next lesson in hand-tool joinery. Making a simple door with unmolded stiles and rails and a flat panel is pretty straightforward. But add a couple of details, and the level of complexity increases by a surprising amount.

These stiles and rails have a typical 18th-century thumbnail molding, and the panel

Build the Bracket Base

MAKE THE SCROLL CUTS IN THE BRACKET BASE. Templates are used to lay out the simple cuts, and a coping saw makes short work of the job. The bracket base is molded, mitered, and attached in much the same way as the cornice.

SEND IN THE REINFORCEMENTS. Corner blocks are nailed and glued on the back to strengthen the base.

Frame-and-Panel Door

The door is the most challenging part: It has a floating raised panel and a thumbnail profile that is coped away at the mortise-and-tenon joints.

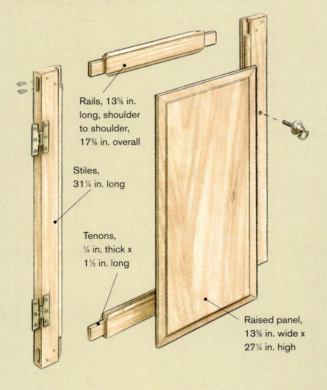

Rails, 13⅝ in. long, shoulder to shoulder, 17⅝ in. overall

Stiles, 31¼ in. long

Tenons, ¼ in. thick x 1½ in. long

Raised panel, 13⅜ in. wide x 27¼ in. high

COPING THE CORNERS

Two edges of the mortise-and-tenon joint are relieved. Then a small amount of the thumbnail edge is coped so that the joint can close.

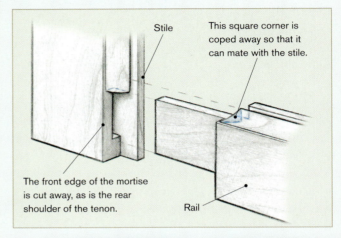

Stile

This square corner is coped away so that it can mate with the stile.

The front edge of the mortise is cut away, as is the rear shoulder of the tenon.

Rail

PLUNGE DOWN WITH A GOUGE TO COPE THE JOINT. Pick a gouge that is close to the radius of the thumbnail and ground along its inside edge.

is raised, or "fielded." Begin by numbering the ends of the mating stiles and rails and then marking the reference edges. As with the face frame, it will be a disaster if your door is too small, so make the stiles and rails oversized. And once again leave the stiles 2 in. longer on each end to support the mortises.

Cut the through-mortises first–
Eighteenth-century passage and entryway doors were typically through-joined, with the joints pinned and wedged rather than glued. These are very effective techniques

for preventing sagging. When you lay out the mortises and tenons, you can use the same setting on your marking gauge that you used for the face frame. Again, use a single reference surface. Lay out the ends of the through-mortise and, with a square, continue the lines over one side and onto the other edge.

Chop the mortise only about halfway through. Then flip over the stile and finish the mortise from the other side. If you are careful to hold your chisels in line with the

CUT THE THUMBNAIL PROFILE. Cut the small fillet with a rabbeting plane, and then round over the thumbnail profile with a block plane, working to a line.

SIGHT DOWN THE SPRING LINES OF A PANEL-RAISING PLANE TO MAINTAIN THE PROPER ANGLE. Cut the cross-grain sides first. Place a waste strip along the back edge to avoid tearout.

AFTER GLUE-UP, THE JOINTS ARE PINNED AND WEDGED. Drive the pins all the way through the door frame before cutting them flush. Then wedge the tenon ends to lock the joint.

workpiece, both cuts should meet in the middle. Wait to cut the tenons.

Plow the grooves–In the 18th century, grooving was done with a plane called a plow. These were and still are made in wood, like mine. They were also made in cast iron. A plow plane features a depth stop and an adjustable fence to control the placement of the groove. Plow planes come with sets of cutters of graduated widths. Be sure to fence the plow against a corresponding face on each rail or stile; otherwise, the grooves may not line up at the corners.

Cut your tenons as you did for the face frame and test their fit. Leave the tenons short of the stile's full width by exactly the depth of the groove. They will not fit all the way through until the molded edge has been cut and coped.

Cut and cope the molding–I have a molding plane that makes a thumbnail. However, you can also use a rabbet plane to create the fillet and a block plane to

round the profile. Use a small profile template to ensure consistent results.

The thumbnail moldings will not come together unless you cope them and cut away the mortise's front edge to the depth of the groove. Coping is a way to make moldings come together at an apparent miter without the problem of the miter opening with seasonal movement. Cope-and-stick router bits undercut the entire tenon shoulder. However, in hand work, it is only necessary to undercut one corner.

To cope the joint you need a gouge close to the same radius as the thumbnail. If the gouge is ground along its inside curve, you can make a clean plunge cut. The thumbnail on the rails and stiles is ½ in., so measure back ½ in. from the shoulder along the molding to locate the top of the cope. The bottom will be at the intersection of the fillet and the shoulder. If your pine is at all crumbly, a straight plunge cut can crush some of the molding and leave a ragged miter. I avoid this by using a slight slicing motion toward the tenon (see "Coping the Corners" on p. 90). Assemble the joint. If your miter is ragged or uneven, you can clean up the coped edge with a sharp chisel. Cope the remaining joints and dry-fit the door. Test for square.

Raise the panel–Cut your panel to size. Remember, this wide panel is intended to float in its frame, permitting seasonal movement. Place a rule in the groove in one stile and measure to the fillet of the opposite thumbnail. This is the maximum width of the panel. If you're building this piece in summer, make the panel about ⅛ in. narrower on each side. In the winter, I suggest

¼ in. per side. The height only needs to be left about ⅛ in. short at each end, regardless of the season.

It is difficult to raise a panel with a standard bench plane; a panel-raising plane makes the job much easier. Antique examples are expensive, but a number of modern makers still produce them (Harris, Crown Plane, Todd Hurley). I have four old models, and each raises a slightly different sized and shaped panel.

A panel raiser is simply a big molding plane that cuts a raised-panel profile, so it is used the same way as a molding plane. It

OPTIONS, OPTIONS. At far left is the cabinet finished with Lexington Green milk paint, with a linseed-oil overcoat. The other version is finished with four washcoats of concentrated tea followed by a tinted shellac.

has a fence and a stop. Keep cutting until the stop comes in contact with the panel. A panel raiser has skewed cutters, which allow the tool to cut cleanly across end grain with a minimum of tearout. Still, choose the best straight-grained pine you have for the panel.

Plane the end grain first, holding the panel between dogs. Place a backer strip at the far corner to prevent break-off. Raising the sides is easier, because you are cutting with the grain.

The trick here is to make each corner come out with a nearly perfect 45° angle. You can make this happen by trimming from one side or the other.

You also can make small adjustments in the fit with a shoulder plane.

Place the panel in the frame and pull the door together with clamps. The panel should not lift up any of the grooved edges. If it does, it is too tight and needs to be planed thinner. Do this by planing the back surface so as not to affect the front.

Assemble the door–Secure all of the joints. The mortises and tenons are pierced by two thin pins. Cut square lengths of pine and whittle them round with a wide, shallow gouge. The slight facets left help lock the pins in place.

The ends of the tenons are wedged at the top and bottom. Again, make squares and whittle the wedges with a gouge. Use a chisel to begin small splits in the tenon ends. Put a very small spot of glue on the wedges and tap them into place. Then saw and plane the wedges flush. These wedges close up the outside of the joint and are an attractive touch.

Trim the horns and plane the door to fit its opening. In the winter, remember to allow for the small amount of expansion that will occur across the stiles.

Two Finish Options

I wanted my cabinet to look as if it had some age. The color I had in mind was the pale tan that raw pine turns to after about five years. However, I did not want to use a stain. Stains darken the softer latewood and leave the harder earlywood lighter in color, which is the opposite of the way pine darkens with age.

I achieved the look I wanted in one afternoon by using nothing more complicated than tea. I made a really strong mixture by steeping three bags in a cup of hot water. When it had cooled, I brushed the strong tea onto the wood, darkening the surface very slightly. I allowed this application to dry and sanded any raised grain. Each subsequent coat of tea darkened the pine further. It took four coats to give me the look I wanted. You can follow with varnish, or if you want to tweak the color slightly—to make it a bit less yellow, for example—use a topcoat of shellac tinted with aniline dye.

Milk paint is another attractive option, and is probably the finish this cabinet would have received in the 1700s. The Old Fashioned Milk Paint Co. is an excellent source for powdered mixes and provides good instructions for their use. A key is to finish the painted surface with linseed oil, which evens out the color.

Hardware

I hung the door with solid brass H-hinges, which are appropriate for an 18th-century design, and I secured the door with a brass pendant latch. Both of these items came from Ball and Ball Hardware Reproductions. While more expensive than the brasses sold at hardware stores and home centers, the prices were not prohibitive. I have always thought it a shame that a woodworker would invest so much in a piece but then install cheap hardware.

MIKE DUNBAR is a contributing editor to *Fine Woodworking* magazine. This article is his third in a sequence of hand-tool-oriented projects.

Sources

Tremont Nail Co.
800-842-0560
www.tremontnail.com

The Old Fashioned Milk Paint Co.
978-448-6336
www.milkpaint.com

Ball and Ball Hardware Reproductions
800-257-3711
www.ballandball-us.com

Craftsman
Wall Cabinet

BY IAN INGERSOLL

There is always a spot for a wall cabinet, especially a small one. This Craftsman-style piece is modeled after a clock, and at a little more than a foot wide it fits well in almost any tight, vertical space. I made it out of butternut, an underused, medium-toned wood that works easily. Because this cabinet was destined for a kitchen, I outfitted the inside to accommodate spices, but the same-sized cabinet could hold anything from pottery to small books. The shelves, in this case, are spaced to fit off-the-rack spice bottles, with the bottom shelf roomy enough for larger, bulk-sized decanters. The tilting drawer at the bottom is made to fit large packages of tea.

When it comes to construction, the simplest answers are often best. On this small, vertical cabinet, I could have dovetailed the case, but I saw no need to spend the time when countersunk and plugged screws would do. And on such a simple piece, I didn't want anything to detract attention from the door, where I spent most of the design and construction energy. I used a flat panel at the bottom of the door to cover the drawer and bulk items, but at the top I installed glass to show off the nicer-looking spice bottles and to make the piece a bit more interesting. Over the

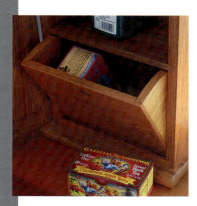

CABINET WITH GLAZED DOOR

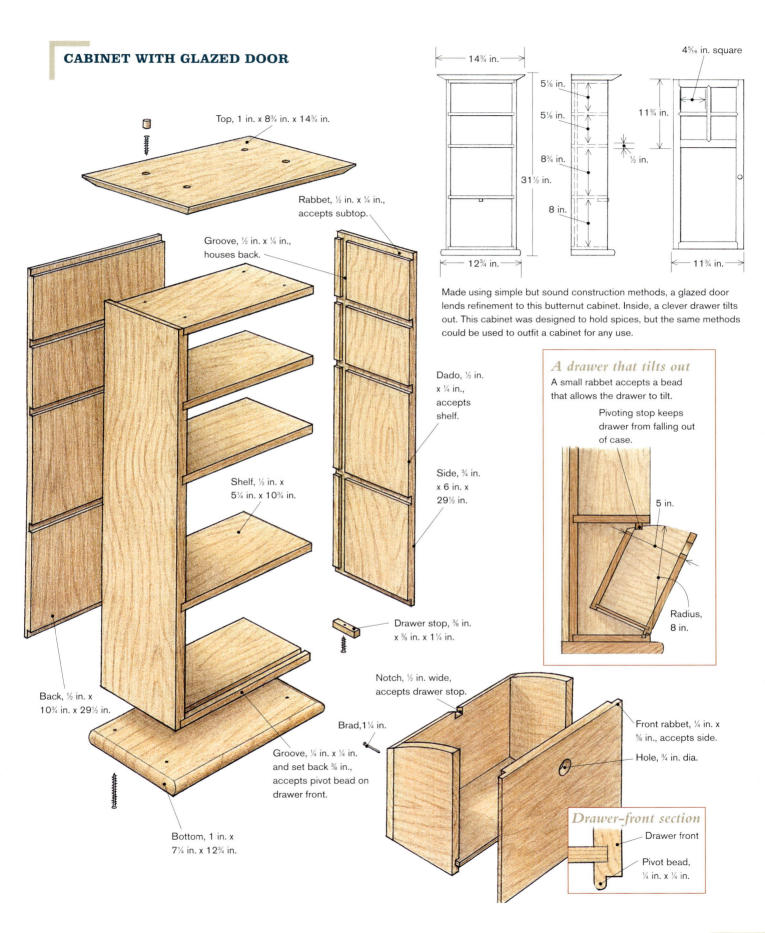

Top, 1 in. x 8¾ in. x 14¾ in.

Rabbet, ½ in. x ¼ in., accepts subtop.

Groove, ½ in. x ¼ in., houses back.

Dado, ½ in. x ¼ in., accepts shelf.

Shelf, ½ in. x 5¼ in. x 10¾ in.

Side, ¾ in. x 6 in. x 29½ in.

Back, ½ in. x 10¾ in. x 29½ in.

Drawer stop, ⅜ in. x ⅜ in. x 1¼ in.

Notch, ½ in. wide, accepts drawer stop.

Brad, 1¼ in.

Groove, ¼ in. x ¼ in. and set back ⅜ in., accepts pivot bead on drawer front.

Bottom, 1 in. x 7¼ in. x 12¾ in.

14¾ in.

4⁵⁄₁₆ in. square

5⅛ in.

5⅛ in.

8¾ in.

11¾ in.

½ in.

31½ in.

8 in.

12¾ in.

11¾ in.

Made using simple but sound construction methods, a glazed door lends refinement to this butternut cabinet. Inside, a clever drawer tilts out. This cabinet was designed to hold spices, but the same methods could be used to outfit a cabinet for any use.

A drawer that tilts out
A small rabbet accepts a bead that allows the drawer to tilt.

Pivoting stop keeps drawer from falling out of case.

5 in.

Radius, 8 in.

Front rabbet, ¼ in. x ⅝ in., accepts side.

Hole, ¾ in. dia.

Drawer-front section
Drawer front

Pivot bead, ¼ in. x ¼ in.

AN EASY AND ELEGANT DOOR

To lend a more elegant look to a simple door, muntins over-lay a single piece of glass, giving the appearance that there are four separate panes.

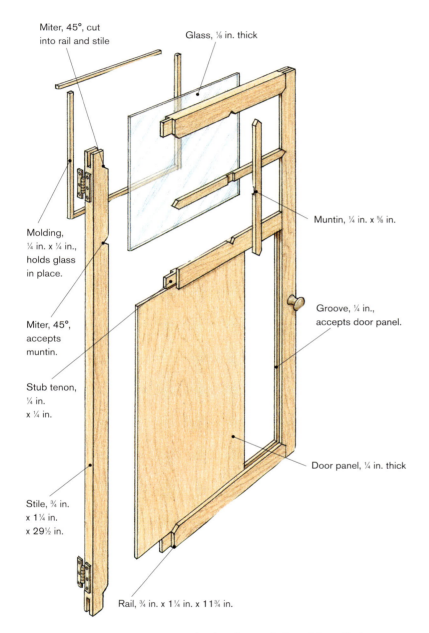

Miter, 45°, cut into rail and stile

Glass, ⅛ in. thick

Molding, ¼ in. x ¼ in., holds glass in place.

Miter, 45°, accepts muntin.

Stub tenon, ¼ in. x ¼ in.

Muntin, ¼ in. x ⅝ in.

Groove, ¼ in., accepts door panel.

Door panel, ¼ in. thick

Stile, ¾ in. x 1¼ in. x 29½ in.

Rail, ¾ in. x 1¼ in. x 11¾ in.

Rear wall of groove is removed to accept glass (above).

shelves are ½ in. thick; the muntins and door panel are ¼ in. thick.

Building the Basic Case

Don't waste energy with overly complex methods of building the case. Use ¾-in.- and ½-in.-thick stock and trim everything to width and length on the tablesaw. Set up the tablesaw to cut ½-in. dadoes for the shelves. Use a stop on your miter gauge to ensure that the dadoes in the back and sides will line up. It's not really necessary to dado the back panel for the shelves, but doing so eases glue-up.

The first step in the process is rabbeting the top and bottom—because the same stop location can be used for each—on all three pieces. Then locate each shelf and set the stop on your miter gauge. When the dadoes have been cut on each of the three pieces, they should all line up perfectly. On the two sides, use the same setup to cut another ½-in. dado, inset ½ in. and ¼ in. deep, to house the back panel.

With the dadoes lined up on the back and sides of the case, trim all of the shelves to width and length and install the ⅜-in.

single piece of glass, I installed muntins, giving the appearance of two-over-two panes of glass.

Begin by milling up the lumber: The top and bottom are 1 in. thick; the sides, door rails, and stiles are ¾ in. thick; the drawer parts are ⅝ in. thick; the back and drawer stop on the bottom shelf. Locate the position by marking off the width of the drawer front, then inset the stop another ³⁄₁₆ in. A screw holds the stop in place and allows it to pivot. On the bottom shelf, cut a ¼-in. by ¼-in. groove with the dado setup on the tablesaw. This groove will work as a hinging mechanism for the tilting drawer. With the drawer stop installed and the groove cut, you can glue up the case, which should go smoothly on such a small piece.

Installing the Top and Bottom

Making the bottom of this case out of 1-in.-thick stock gives the piece a grounded look. Just remember to leave a ½-in. overhang on the front and sides, and make sure you account for the door. Rout a 1-in. bullnose on the edges of the bottom and leave the decoration for the top.

The treatment for the top is one I regularly use on tabletops. It lends the piece a nice, finished look and helps draw your attention to the glass panels in the door. Start by cutting a ¼-in. bead on the outside edge at the front and sides. Then establish the overhang, in this case 1½ in., and mark a line there. If it feels safe, use the tablesaw. With the piece held upright, sight down the raised blade and adjust the angle until it enters at the bottom of the bead and exits at the overhang line. You can achieve the same results by cutting to the line with a handplane. The result is a rounded top edge that angles back sharply toward the case. Both the top and bottom are simply screwed onto the case and pegged.

Building the Drawer

When you open this case, the drawer at the bottom is a nice surprise. Instead of sliding as a normal drawer would, this tall drawer tilts forward and down so that you can reach in for tea or whatever you decide to store inside. The sides and back are rounded so that the drawer slides open

Setting Mutins in Place

PANES FOR THE GLASS. With two 45° cuts on each muntin end, the muntins are laid in place, and the miters are marked on the rails and stiles.

CUTTING MITERS IN THE RAILS AND STILES. To accept the muntin ends, a small gentleman's saw cuts miters on the door frame.

CROSSING THE GLASS. To give the appearance of divided panes of glass, muntins are added. The half-lap joint is cut on the tablesaw.

Making an Easy Bridle Joint

AN EASY BUT REFINED DOOR DETAIL.
With the rail grooved and the mortise cut,
a bandsaw trims away the inside edge to
accept the stile.

A MITERED DOOR JOINT. With a 45° miter
jig clamped to the rail, a chisel pares to
the line. This simple detail lends a framed
and finished look to the door.

A PERFECT FIT. It's best to work out any
problems before you begin glue-up. A dry
run ensures that everything fits and that
the bridle joints pull tight.

easily with the pull—nothing more than a
¾-in.-dia. hole in the front—but the stop
keeps the drawer from falling out on the
floor. By twisting the stop you can easily
remove the whole drawer for easy cleaning or restocking.

The four sides of the drawer are cut to
size and dadoed with a ¼-in. blade to accept
the plywood bottom. Make sure you cut
the front ¼ in. wider so that there will be
enough material to form the pivoting bead
along the bottom. The side edges of the
front and back are rabbeted to accept the
sides. The two sides and the back are all
shaped on the bandsaw, and a small notch is
removed from the top center of the back to
allow for the drawer stop.

To provide the tilting action, the bottom of the front of the drawer has a ¼-in.
bead that protrudes down into the groove
cut into the bottom of the case. Rout this
bead on the inside of the drawer front,
then use a dado blade to remove the front

edge. This bead should fit nicely into the
groove on the bottom of the case and
allow the drawer to fall forward. The
drawer is glued up with the bottom floating in the dadoes, and a few brads in the
sides and back hold everything in place.

Building and Glazing the Door

The bulk of the work on this small piece
involves the cabinet's natural focal point: the
door. First, cut the rails and stiles to 1¼ in.
wide and trim them to length. Use bridle
joints to frame the door. Bridle joints not
only offer plenty of strength, but they also
make easy work of measuring. Because the
tenons run the full width of the door, simply mark the length of each piece off the
case itself. The center rail is the one exception, and it is cut with small tenons that fit
into ¼-in. by ¼-in. grooves on the stiles.

By cutting the tenons and mortises 1 in.
deep instead of 1¼ in. deep (the full width

of the rails and stiles), you leave material to cut the 45° haunches at the joints. These haunched tenons not only look more refined, but they also allow you to rip the rail and stile grooves full length on the tablesaw.

Use a ¼-in. dado setup to cut the grooves on the inside faces of the rails and stiles. For the median and upper rails, you also remove the inside portion of the groove so that the glass can slide into place after the door has been assembled.

Using the same dado setup and a simple jig that fits over the tablesaw to hold the stiles upright, raise the blade to 1 in. and cut a tenon slot on the ends of the rails. Adjust the fence so that in two passes you're able to leave the ¼-in.-thick tenon. At the bandsaw, trim down the width on the inside of the tenon by ¼ in. You'll notice that this leaves the tenon length ¼ in. shy of mating correctly. A simple miter jig clamped onto the rails and stiles helps guide the chisel for the 45° cuts.

Once you've milled and trimmed a center panel for the bottom of the door, the door can be glued up. When the glue dries, you'll still have to remove the inside of the groove on the upper portion of the door

where the glass will be installed. Do this with a straightedge and a box knife, then clean it up with a chisel. The final touch to this door is to install the muntins. Cut them ⅝ in. wide and center them on the square upper portion of the door. Then use a small gentleman's saw to cut the 45° miters that accommodate the muntins. Once the two pieces press-fit into place, lay one across the other and mark the centers. Cut a ⅛-in. groove where the two cross each other. When installed, a few drops of glue at the groove and on the mitered ends, along with a little tension from the door itself, hold everything in place.

Once the glass slides in, small pieces of molding are used to secure it. All that's left to do is to hang the door and apply the finish and hardware. I used an oil varnish from Waterlox to give this piece a natural look and to provide protection. The hinges I used are antiqued, solid brass H-hinges from Horton Brass, and the knob is a Shaker-style bronze knob from Colonial Bronze. After you're done, open the cabinet, reach in the drawer, and fix yourself a cup of tea.

IAN INGERSOLL designs and builds furniture in West Cornwall, Conn.

Sources

Horton Brass
860-635-4400

Colonial Bronze
860-489-9233

Magazine Cabinet

BY CHRIS GOCHNOUR

Like many woodworkers I know, my shop and resource library are in different locations. My detached garage serves as my shop, but I keep books and my collection of *Fine Woodworking* magazines stored in a bookcase in the basement of the house. My workshop doesn't have a shelf or cabinet big enough to store

them all. I finally decided to do something about the problem and set out to design and build a cabinet deserving of the body of knowledge I've gained from *Fine Woodworking.*

The cabinet would have to hold more than 25 years, or 100 lb., of magazines, so it had to be sturdy. I also needed it to be compact. There's not a lot of empty wall space in my shop. And most of all, I wanted the design to be minimal, something that would let beautiful wood and simple form speak for themselves and blend in nicely with my nearby tool-storage cabinets.

Durable Joinery is Critical

I constructed the cabinet using two durable joints: through-dovetails (to attach the top to the sides) and wedged mortise and tenons (to attach the bottom to the sides). A piece of cove molding, cut on the tablesaw, serves as a crown and obscures the dovetails, which I cut quickly using a Leigh jig.

There were two reasons for using wedged mortise and tenons on the base. One, I wanted a continuous line with a slight overhang at the base of the cabinet. That ruled out using through-dovetails. Second, I wanted the cabinet to be tough. A wedged mortise-and-tenon joint is very

WALL-MOUNTED CABINET CAN HANDLE A HEAVY LOAD

Made of cherry and spalted maple and constructed using through-dovetails on top and wedged mortise and tenons at the base, the cabinet can withstand heavy loads (146 issues of *Fine Woodworking* weigh more than 100 lb.). A French cleat provides secure mounting to a wall.

2⅛ in.

1½ in.

¾ in.

¼ in.

¾ in.   ³⁄₁₆ in.

Cove molding

Case top, ¾ in. x 11¾ in. x 23 in., is dovetailed to sides.

Mortise for cleat, ¼ in. wide x ½ in. deep x 11¹⁵⁄₁₆ in. long

All rails and stiles, ½ in. thick x 2¾ in. wide

French cleat is mortised into sides of case.

8⅞ in. from top of door to center of rail

Shelf, 9½ in. deep x 21⅞ in. wide (include ¼-in.-long tenons)

Back fits into ½-in.-wide x ³⁄₁₆-in.-deep dado on sides, top, and bottom.

Doors, 11½ in. x 26¾ in.

Knife hinges are ½ in. wide.

Haunched tenons, ¼ in. thick x 2¹⁄₁₆ in. wide x ¾ in. deep

Back panels, ½ in. thick, are rabbeted on both sides (⅜ in. wide x ⅛ in. deep).

Case side, ¾ in. thick x 10⅞ in. wide x 28⅜ in. high

The bottom, ¾ in. thick x 11⅞ in. wide x 23⅜ in. long, is fitted to the sides using wedged mortise-and-tenon joints.

³⁄₁₆-in. overhang

28⅜ in.

23⅜ in.

2½ in.

Wedged Mortise and Tenons Step by Step

Wedges are driven into slotted tenons that fit into tapered mortises. In cross section, this joint re-sembles a dovetail. When making the wedges (left), set the miter gauge on the tablesaw to 3°, cut one side, then flip the stock and rip off a wedge.

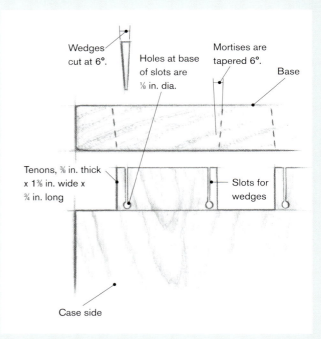

Wedges cut at 6°.

Holes at base of slots are ⅛ in. dia.

Mortises are tapered 6°.

Base

Tenons, ⅜ in. thick x 1⅜ in. wide x ¾ in. long

Slots for wedges

Case side

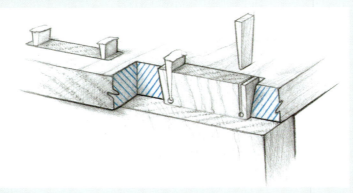

1. START BY CUTTING TAPERED MORTISES

CUT THROUGH-MORTISES. Cut halfway through one side, then flip the stock and finish from the other side to avoid tearout.

MARK THE TAPERS FOR THE MORTISES. Use a bevel gauge set for 6° and mark the edge, then transfer the marks to the bottom face with a square.

WORKING FROM THE BOTTOM, TAPER THE EDGES OF EACH MORTISE. The author uses a guide block, cut at 6°, and a chisel the same width as the mortise.

2. LOCATE THE TENONS FROM THE MORTISES

MACHINE ONE LONG TENON ON EACH SIDE OF THE CASE. The author cuts the tenons slightly deeper than the mortises; the excess will be trimmed off after the glue-up.

MARK OFF THE INDIVIDUAL TENONS. Use the already mortised base as a guide.

CUT SLOTS IN THE TENONS. Each tenon receives two slots. When wedges are driven, the tenons flare out, creating a secure joint.

3. GLUE UP THE CASE BOTTOM LAST

SPREAD GLUE ON THE SURFACES OF THE MORTISES, TENONS, AND WEDGES. Gently tap the wedges in place. Clamps hold the carcase together. After the glue dries, trim the wedges. A flush-cutting saw makes the job easier.

IN THE FIRST GLUE-UP, THE SIDES ARE JOINED TO THE TOP, BACK, AND SHELF. It's less stressful to leave the bottom for last and not have to worry about trying to get everything done at once before the glue sets.

Spalted Panels Highlight Simple Doors

To achieve a visual balance, the lower rails are wider than the upper rails. And the pulls are centered in relation to the lower panels.

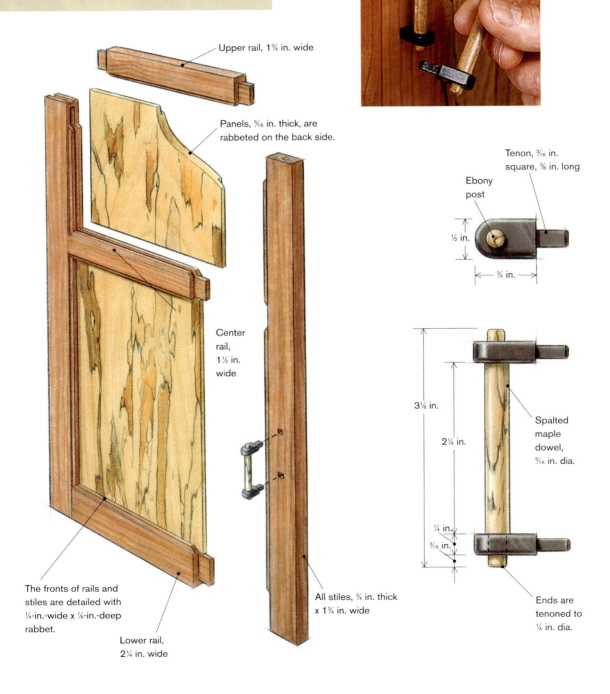

Upper rail, 1¾ in. wide

Panels, ⁵⁄₁₆ in. thick, are rabbeted on the back side.

Center rail, 1½ in. wide

The fronts of rails and stiles are detailed with ¼-in.-wide x ⅛-in.-deep rabbet.

Lower rail, 2¼ in. wide

All stiles, ¾ in. thick x 1¾ in. wide

Tenon, ³⁄₁₆ in. square, ⅜ in. long

Ebony post

½ in.

¾ in.

3⅛ in.

2¼ in.

¼ in.

³⁄₁₆ in.

Spalted maple dowel, ⁵⁄₁₆ in. dia.

Ends are tenoned to ¼ in. dia.

The pulls, made of spalted maple and ebony, complement the color and grain found in the panels.

DOWELS CAN BE MADE ON THE ROUTER TABLE. Take two passes, leaving the end of the stock unmilled, to provide a flat, stable support.

BEGIN WITH AN EBONY BLANK ¾ IN. THICK BY ¾ IN. WIDE AND 12 IN. LONG. Rout the ends with a ¼-in. radius roundover bit. The adjoining piece prevents tearout.

CUT ⁵⁄₁₆-IN. SQUARE TENONS ON THE POSTS. Each blank is good for two posts, one on each end.

strong, even if the glue fails. Sliding dovetails also would have worked, but I wanted something different. Wedged mortise and tenons work mechanically like dovetails, because the tenons are flared to fit tapered mortises (see the drawings on p. 102). One could certainly use this joint at the top of the case, but it takes a little longer than cutting dovetails using a router jig. Before laying out and cutting the mortises and tenons for the base, I completed all of the joinery at the top, then dry-fit the assembly.

I cut the mortises using a hollow-chisel mortiser. To minimize tearout, I cut halfway through one side, flipped the stock, and then finished cutting from the other side. When all of the mortises had been chopped, I beveled them 6° using a guide block and a sharp chisel.

Next, I began cutting single, full-length tenons on the tablesaw. Then I positioned the tenoned sides against the mortised base and marked off the locations of the individual tenons. The tenons were cut using a

backsaw and a coping saw, and I cleaned them up with a chisel. All of the tenons were slotted to receive a pair of wedges.

Cutting the wedges gave me the opportunity to do something odd: rip stock using a miter gauge. The wedges were made from an offcut, from the end of a board; the wedges can be of the same species as the cabinet (what I did) or of a contrasting species. I set the miter gauge to 3° and took one pass, technically a ripping cut, then flipped over the stock and took another pass to make a 6° wedge. For safety I used a zero-clearance throat plate.

Back and Shelf Sit in Grooves

With the basic carcase joinery completed, grooves must be milled to receive the cabinet back and shelf. (Refer to the drawing on p. 101 to see which grooves are stopped and which can safely be run through.) The fact that the frame-and-panel back fits into grooves is a bit unusual because backs are typically installed in rabbets. But because

Hanging Doors with Knife Hinges

MORTISE THE DOORS AND ATTACH THE KNIFE HINGES. Note that the pivot pin must be located beyond the door's edge. Use waxed steel screws to cut the wood fibers. Later, replace them with the delicate brass screws.

YOU NEED A SLIGHT GAP BETWEEN THE DOOR AND EDGE OF CASE. The author uses a 1/16-in.-thick ruler as a shim, then transfers the location of the knife hinges.

ROUT KNIFE-HINGE MORTISES IN THE CASE. It's much easier to cut mortises before gluing up the carcase. The author used a router plane.

this cabinet attaches to the wall using a ¾-in.-thick French cleat, I had to move the back into the case by that amount. Also, I wanted to fit the French cleat to the case using mortise-and-tenon joints. Cutting a deep rabbet would have left me without enough wood to cut a good mortise. So I went with shallow grooves to house the back, which makes glue-up a little tricky. More on that later.

The shelf sits in a stopped dado cut into the sides of the cabinet. It is set back slightly from the front of the case. The shelf must also be tenoned.

Traditional Frame-and-Panel Doors with Handmade Pulls

The doors are classic frame-and-panel construction and are hung on knife hinges. I cut a very slight rabbet on the faces of the rails and stiles, where they meet the panels (see the drawings on p. 104), to produce

delicate shadow lines. The final touch is a pair of shopmade pulls.

The pulls are spalted-maple dowels, tenoned at each end, attached to the doors using ebony posts, also tenoned. Although a lathe could be used, I chose to shape the dowels on my router table. I simply made two passes over a 5/16-in.-dia. bead cutter and did a little sanding. To shape the tenons on the ends of the dowels, I used a plug cutter, mounted in a drill press.

I needed only a sliver of ebony to make the posts, but I used a piece that was long enough to be milled safely. The stock had to be milled in steps, then ripped into narrower pieces, then machined again. I was surprised at how much work went into these parts. When done, I slipped the dowels into the posts and glued the posts into mortises chopped in the stiles of the doors.

Mounting the doors–Knife hinges are a little tricky to install, because they are mortised into the case and doors. To install the hinges, I first dry-assembled the cabinet. I put the hinges on the doors, then placed the doors against the case and marked the locations of the hinges. To take into account the gap between the door and the edge of the case when marking the hinge locations, I used a 1/16-in.-thick ruler as a shim. Then I disassembled the cabinet and cut knife-hinge mortises into the cabinet top and bottom.

The Cabinet Hangs on a French Cleat

A French cleat (also called beveled cleat) is a very sound way of securing a cabinet to a wall (see p. 114). The method employs two interlocking pieces. One cleat is attached to the top of the cabinet back and the other to the wall. A cabinet is simply hung over the cleat, and gravity keeps it from going anywhere. There are no ugly screws to mar the inside of the cabinet, and it's easy to move or relocate the piece should you decide to do so.

Any hardwood will do for the cleat. I chose maple because of its toughness. I strengthened the cleat by attaching it to the cabinet using mortise-and-tenon joinery. The cleat mounted to the wall must be securely fastened to studs using lag bolts or two #12 by 3-in. screws per stud.

Don't Glue Up the Carcase All at Once

The glue-up of this cabinet poses a few challenges. To buy a little extra time on this complex glue-up, I use Titebond Extend wood glue. I broke down the glue-up into two phases, because even this glue would not give me enough time to complete the entire job. First, I glued up the dovetails, the back, the beveled cleat and the shelf. To help keep the carcase square, I dry-fitted the base in place and let the assembly dry for several hours.

Once the glue set, I glued the base in place. I used clamps to ensure that the tenons would seat themselves, then coated the wedges with glue and drove them home. Once the wedges have been driven, you're at the point of no return: The case will not come apart, so the clamps may be removed. Once the glue dried, I cut off the protruding wedges and planed the tenons flush with the base.

Oil and Lacquer Finish Is Sprayed On

I chose an oil and lacquer finish for the cabinet because the oil brings out the richness and depth of the wood, and the lacquer produces a nice luster.

Spalted maple can be a difficult wood to finish. It is, after all, slightly rotted, and it often suffers from soft, punky areas that absorb finish at different rates, creating an uneven sheen. To get around that problem, I finished the maple panels first by spraying on numerous coats of lacquer, sanding between coats, until the finish built up to an even sheen.

For the cherry, I used clear Watco oil, thinned 50 percent with naphtha to speed up drying. Naphtha outperforms paint thinner because it's a faster-drying solvent. I sprayed the entire cabinet with this mixture (don't worry; when the lacquer is dry, the oil won't harm it), then wiped down the piece and let it dry overnight.

The following day I sprayed on two thin coats of lacquer, which gave me the luster I wanted without the effort of a rubbed-out oil finish. The finish was dry to the touch a few hours later, but for peace of mind I waited a day or two for it to cure before filling up the cabinet with my collection of *Fine Woodworking* magazines.

CHRIS GOCHNOUR builds custom furniture in Salt Lake City, Utah.

Wineglass Cabinet

BY SCOTT GIBSON

Wall cabinets are relatively small. That's one of their beauties. They can be used in many spaces that would be too cramped for larger pieces of furniture, and their scale makes them familiar and approachable. A wall cabinet also can be made from scraps and offcuts of prized lumber that would be unusable elsewhere.

Wall cabinets lend themselves to many variations in design, depending on where they will be installed and what they will be used for. This cabinet is made of quarter-sawn white ash. It is for wineglasses and is

TAPERED STILES and glass panels lighten an ash cabinet.

BASE MOLDING SUPPORTS THE CABINET

This simple box is accented by doors with tapered stiles, which gives the illusion that the piece has a slight V-shape. The cornice and the matching base also provide some weight to the piece and reinforce the tapered appearance.

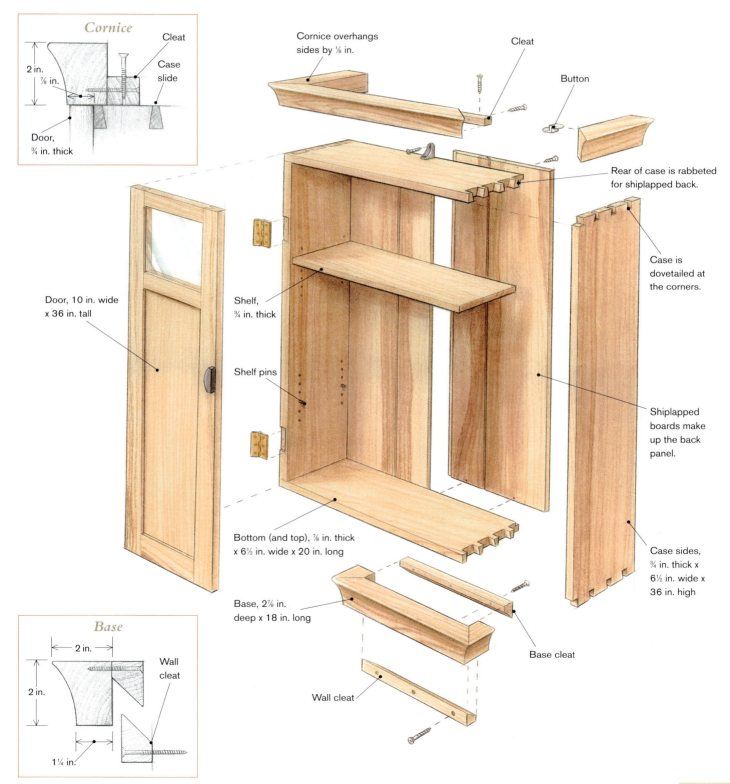

Cornice

2 in.

⅞ in.

Cleat

Case slide

Door, ¾ in. thick

Cornice overhangs sides by ⅛ in.

Cleat

Button

Rear of case is rabbeted for shiplapped back.

Case is dovetailed at the corners.

Door, 10 in. wide x 36 in. tall

Shelf, ¾ in. thick

Shelf pins

Shiplapped boards make up the back panel.

Bottom (and top), ⅞ in. thick x 6½ in. wide x 20 in. long

Case sides, ¾ in. thick x 6½ in. wide x 36 in. high

Base, 2⅞ in. deep x 18 in. long

Base cleat

Wall cleat

Base

2 in.

2 in.

1¼ in.

Wall cleat

Doors with Tapered Stiles Require Careful Planning

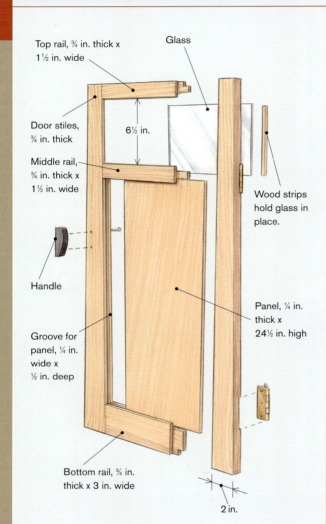

Top rail, ¾ in. thick x 1½ in. wide

Glass

Door stiles, ¾ in. thick

6½ in.

Middle rail, ¾ in. thick x 1½ in. wide

Wood strips hold glass in place.

Handle

Panel, ¼ in. thick x 24½ in. high

Groove for panel, ¼ in. wide x ½ in. deep

Bottom rail, ¾ in. thick x 3 in. wide

2 in.

Top rail

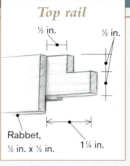

½ in.   ½ in.

Rabbet, ½ in. x ½ in.   1¼ in.

Middle rail

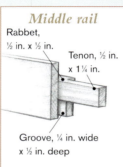

Rabbet, ½ in. x ½ in.

Tenon, ½ in. x 1¼ in.

Groove, ¼ in. wide x ½ in. deep

Bottom rail

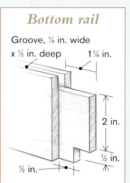

Groove, ¼ in. wide x ½ in. deep   1¼ in.

2 in.

½ in.

½ in.

1. TAPER THE STILES

Use a jig to cut the 1° taper. Save the offcuts because you'll need them to help cut the rails.

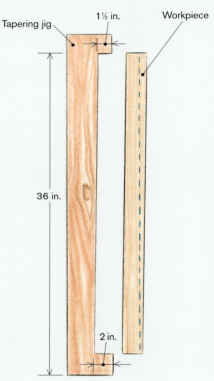

Tapering jig   1½ in.   Workpiece

36 in.

2 in.

intended for a dining room. It is less than 7 in. deep. With the exceptions of the cornice and the matching base, the cabinet is rectilinear. Door stiles are tapered slightly on the inside edge to help the cabinet appear lighter at the top. A coved cornice gives the top of the case some heft, and small windows at the tops of the doors give you a peek inside. There's minimal hardware, so the wood is really what's on display.

Size the Cabinet to Fit the Glasses

Unless the cabinet has no specific use, it makes sense to size it carefully for the things that are to be stored there. Wineglasses come in many sizes and shapes, but those in the mixed collection my wife and I own are about 3½ in. wide and about 7 in. tall. Those dimensions became the rough guide for laying out the cabinet. Although

2. TENON THE RAILS

Tack portions of offcuts from the stiles onto a crosscut sled for your tablesaw. Place the thicker ends near the blade.

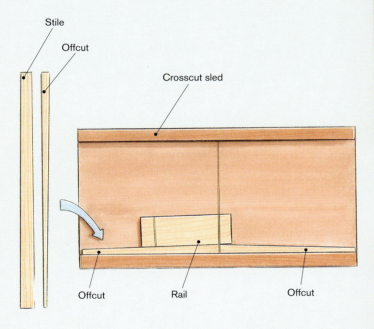

Stile

Offcut

Crosscut sled

Offcut

Rail

Offcut

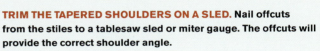

TRIM THE TAPERED SHOULDERS ON A SLED. Nail offcuts from the stiles to a tablesaw sled or miter gauge. The offcuts will provide the correct shoulder angle.

FIT THE MIDDLE RAIL. Dry-fit the door frame and fit the middle rail to the piece, using a full-sized drawing as a guide.

adjustable shelves allow some flexibility in height, there is no way to fudge a cabinet that is too shallow.

There are two other considerations: the thickness of the back, which is set into rabbets in the back of the case, and whether the doors will be inset or overlay. The back of this cabinet was made from four shiplapped boards. A frame-and-panel back was another good option, but shiplapping these boards was the best way to present the

bands of browns and creams in the wood. Because the boards were set into the back of the case, the overall depth of the cabinet had to be increased by at least that much. I added a safety margin of another ½ in. in case we ever get slightly larger glasses.

If you choose inset doors—those that fit inside the case—they also must be factored into the depth of the case. Doors should be a full ¾ in. thick, so the sides of the case

Coved Cornice

1. CUT THE COVE ON THE TABLESAW

Make a ¾-in.-deep cove by taking very light cuts across the blade. It should take about six to 10 passes.

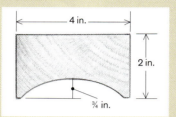

SET YOUR GUIDE 2 IN. FROM THE CROWN OF THE BLADE. This cut will be made at 45°.

CUT THE COVE. Move the stock over the blade at a slow but steady pace. Don't remove too much with each cut.

2. RIP, MITER, AND ATTACH THE CORNICE

RIP TO SIZE. Determine the height you want the cornice to be and rip it to width.

TRIANGULAR BLOCKS ADD BITE TO SPRING-CLAMP JAWS TO CLOSE UP MITERS. Attach the blocks with hot-melt glue, and chisel them off after the cornice is dry.

ATTACH THE CORNICE TO THE CASE. The front cornice piece is screwed through the cleat. The side pieces are attached with buttons, which allow for wood movement.

must be that much wider if this is the door style you choose. I chose overlay doors, which are attached to the outside edges of the case. One visual advantage of overlay doors is that they give the case a cleaner, less cluttered look—from the front, you see the doors, not the edges of the case. Another option is to make the top and bottom of the case wider than the sides by the thickness of the door. This allows the doors to cover the edges of the cabinet sides but fit inside the top and bottom pieces.

As for width, I wanted to fit five or six glasses side by side on each shelf. A little extra room here also is a good idea.

The carcase is just a four-sided box, dovetailed at the corners. The sides are ¾ in. thick, and the top and the bottom are ⅞ in. thick. Although using half-blind dovetails would have kept the sides of the case cleaner, I'm still a sucker for at least some exposed joinery, so I used through-dovetails. I made the top a little thicker to allow slightly longer pins (these are cut with a 1:8 angle).

Doors Are the Focal Point

This cabinet is almost all door, so it pays to use the best wood you have for the panels and the door parts. I liked the idea of a cabinet that was tapered—slightly narrower at the top than at the bottom. But that seemed to create more problems than were worth solving, so I opted instead to taper the inside edges of the door stiles. The taper is gentle—about 1°—going from 2 in. wide at the bottom of each stile to 1½ in. wide at the top. A more severe taper would have made the stile too wide at the bottom or too narrow at the top to accommodate a tenon. Each door also was fitted with a trapezoidal window roughly 7 in. on a side.

The easiest way to lay out the mortise-and-tenon joints for the door was to use a full-sized drawing on a piece of paper or scrap of plywood. The length of each of the three rails was taken directly from the

drawing. I just had to add an allowance for the tenons.

After cutting the rails to size, I made the cheek cuts on the tablesaw using a simple jig. Then I finished the tenons with the rails flat on a tablesaw sled. To get the right angle, I took the offcuts left over from tapering the door stiles and tacked them to the tablesaw sled. If the joints didn't fit perfectly, I adjusted them with a shoulder plane or put them back on the jig to remove a little more wood with the tablesaw. Making the door parts and dry-fitting them directly on the full-sized template simplified the process. But it did take

Wall cabinets lend themselves to many variations in design.

THIS CABINET, designed for a dining room, can be sized to fit different-sized glasses.

some fussing to get three unequally sized rails into place while keeping the stiles parallel and the door square.

The little windows fit in a rabbet cut in the back of the middle rail, the top rail, and the two stiles. This was a good place for a router. The rabbet can be created using a bearing-guided rabbeting bit after the door has been glued up. Small strips of wood hold the glass in place. They can be secured either with brads or with hot-melt glue.

Coved Cornice Can be Cut on a Tablesaw

I don't own a shaper, but by passing the stock at an angle over the tablesaw blade, I was able to produce the coved cornices for this cabinet with ease. By varying the angle of the approach and the angle of the blade, this technique allows you to make profiles of amazing variety—from plain semicircular cuts to dramatic shapes that look like waves about to break. The trick is to clamp guides

A FRENCH CLEAT BEARS THE WEIGHT. The base engages with the wall cleat, and the cabinet sits atop the base. The case requires only a single screw at the top to hold it securely to the wall.

to the tablesaw so that the stock won't wander and to take $\frac{1}{16}$-in. or smaller bites.

The stock for the cornice was 2 in. thick, giving me plenty of material in which to cut the profile. After cutting the cove in the center of the material, I ripped one edge to give the cornice its finished shape. The pieces were mitered and glued together as a unit before they were attached to the case. By hot-gluing triangular-shaped blocks on the two outside corners, I was able to use spring clamps to close the miter tightly. When gluing up the assembly, a spacer block can be inserted between the two short legs, if necessary, to keep the assembly in shape. I cleaned up the saw marks on the pieces before gluing them together.

Once the glue dried, I sanded the corners to remove any traces of squeeze-out and screwed the assembly to the top of the case. The front edge of the assembly overhangs the front of the case by about $\frac{7}{8}$ in. The overhang covers the tops of the doors and allows for a small lip. A cleat attached to the back of the front cornice was screwed to the top of the case; on the two short legs of the cornice, tabletop buttons made a tight connection while allowing for cross-grain seasonal movement in the case top. Attached this way, the front of the cornice won't move.

There is one other component made with the same material—the base that supports the cabinet on the wall. It is only $2\frac{7}{8}$ in. deep, enough to give the cabinet a sturdy shelf but shallow enough that it doesn't make the cabinet look bottom-heavy. It is 4 in. narrower than the cabinet. After the three sides of the base piece were joined, I added a base cleat that meshes with a corresponding cleat screwed to the wall. Called a French cleat, this hanging system hides any fasteners, and it is simple to install and remove.

Hang the Doors and Apply a Finish

Depending on how the case is built, knife hinges would be a good choice for this cabinet. They are unobtrusive and strong. I've also used crank hinges (Whitechapel Hardware), which allow doors to be folded open all the way. I decided on good-quality extruded brass butt hinges.

Because the cabinet has overlay doors, the stops are already built in. To keep the doors closed, I used small, powerful magnets sold by Lee Valley. They are less difficult to install than conventional bullet catches and will be unaffected by small seasonal changes in the doors.

Fitting overlay doors is not as finicky as fitting inset doors, but the outside edge of each door still should line up exactly with the edge of the case. Planing a bevel of a degree or two on the mating edges of the center stiles makes it easier to open and close the doors without having them bind.

For finish, a coat of Watco oil brings out the wood's color, and three or four coats of blond shellac or lacquer protect it.

SCOTT GIBSON is a freelance writer living in Maine. He is the author of *The Workshop*.

Sources

Lee Valley
P.O. Box 1780
Ogdensburg, NY
13669-6780
800-871-8158
www.leevalley.com for
more locations

Whitechapel Hardware
P.O. Box 11719
Jackson, WY 83002
307-739-9478
www.Whitechapel-Ltd.com

Build a Shaker Round Stand

BY CHRIS BECKSVOORT

Having built almost 70 round stands, I still continue to revise and refine the shape and dimensions in an effort to achieve the perfect shape. The Shakers built a variety of round stands. They were conveniently placed near reading chairs, desks, worktables, benches, and beds because the Shakers did all after-dark work by candlelight. That's why round stands are often called candle stands. Although crude at first, the designs became more refined and delicate during the early 19th century.

The pinnacle of round-stand design was achieved by a Shaker craftsman from Hancock, Mass., in the first half of the 1800s. The original stand is now in New York's Metropolitan Museum of Art. The stand consists of a ½-in.-thick by 18-in.-dia. top with a rounded edge, and the stand's tabletop is attached to the post by a cross brace. The post is a 3-in.-dia. turning resembling a wine bottle, with a ⅛-in. indentation at the bottom to accept the legs. The post is topped with a tulip swelling that has a round tenon to fit into the cross brace. The legs are a smooth cyma curve flowing out of the post with an arched curve below. The

THE PINNACLE OF ROUND-STAND DESIGN is reflected in this table based on a piece built by a Shaker craftsman from Hancock, Mass., circa 1830. Whether as a side table, end table, night stand, or reading lamp stand, the smooth, flowing lines of this stand will brighten any room.

SHAKER ROUND STAND

This drawing is the author's interpretation of an original Shaker round stand built in the first half of the 1800s at Hancock, Mass. The original is now in the Metropolitan Museum of Art in New York City.

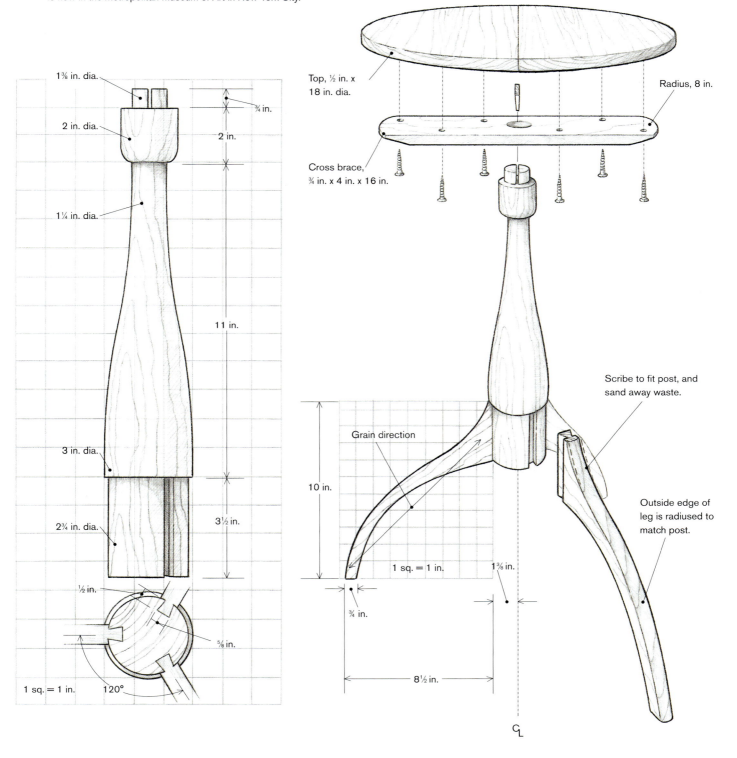

1⅜ in. dia.

2 in. dia.

1¼ in. dia.

¾ in.

2 in.

11 in.

3 in. dia.

2¾ in. dia.

3½ in.

½ in.

⅝ in.

1 sq. = 1 in.   120°

Top, ½ in. x 18 in. dia.

Radius, 8 in.

Cross brace, ¾ in. x 4 in. x 16 in.

Scribe to fit post, and sand away waste.

Grain direction

10 in.

1 sq. = 1 in.   1⅜ in.

¾ in.

8½ in.

Outside edge of leg is radiused to match post.

Leg tapers from ¾ in. thick at top to ½ in. thick at bottom.

Router Makes Quick Work of Sliding Dovetails

As a teacher, I often suggest a round stand as a first project for beginning students. The stand's small scale and frugal use of materials make it approachable, and the level of complexity in several processes, including hand-cutting the sliding dovetails, makes it a nearly perfect project for the novice. Also, the students always appreciate the attractive piece of furniture they walk away with.

As one who believes teaching by example is sound, I, too, would cut the joints by hand. That is, until I was faced with having to make three stands in short order. To speed up production, I developed a lathe-mounted jig (see the photo below)

that let me cut accurate and repeatable dovetail sockets with a router.

CONSTRUCTING THE JIG. I constructed the jig with medium-density fiberboard (MDF) because of its stability and flatness. Other materials may be used; however, avoid solid stock because of its propensity to move. It is vital that the jig's pieces be square and accurate so that the router riding on top of the jig cuts parallel to the centerline of the lathe.

I began by cutting two pieces of MDF for the sides of the jig. The height of the jig needs to be equal to the swing of your lathe and at least one-half the diameter of the

spindle you are turning. The length is limited by the length of the project mounted in the lathe. I cut a dado for the bottom of the jig about 1 in. up from the lower edge of the side. The width of the bottom depends on the width of your lathe bed. On the underside of the bottom, I milled a shallow dado equal in width to the gap in the lathe bed. Into this dado, I fit another block of MDF that acts as a key to permit the assembled jig to slide along the bed of the lathe in line with the axis of the lathe centers.

I glued and screwed the jig together, checking carefully to be sure the sides were square to the

CUTTING SLIDING DOVETAIL SOCKETS IS A SIMPLE TASK WITH THIS LATHE-MOUNTED JIG. The jig must be square, accurate, and parallel to the axis of the lathe for proper attachment of the legs. The stability of medium-density fiberboard makes it a good choice for jigs.

TO CUT THE DOVETAIL SOCKETS, the router rides on top of the jig, with an edge guide positioned to center the bit on the table post. The author first hogs out most of the socket waste with a straight bit and finally cuts the socket in one pass with a dovetail bit.

bottom. Once positioned, I added a few braces to hold the sides square. After the glue dried, I drilled a hole through the bottom of the jig for the bolt that clamps the jig to the lathe bed.

USING THE JIG. To use the jig, I unplugged the lathe and clamped the jig to the lathe bed. My lathe has an indexing headstock, so I can lock the turning in position. If your lathe doesn't have a built-in indexing system, it's fairly easy to add a shop-built indexing wheel to the headstock.

I positioned the router so its bit would be at top dead center of the turning, and I adjusted the router's edge guide to ride along the side of the jig to control the cut. I chucked a straight bit in the router and then cut flats on the turning where the legs will butt against the post. The width of the flat needs to be just a hair wider than the thickness of the leg. After cutting the first flat, I rotated the turning 120°, repeated the process for the second flat, and again for the third flat.

With the flats cut, I wasted away the bulk of the joint in two or three passes with a ½-in.-dia. straight bit, indexing the head as before. I completed the socket by switching to a dovetail bit and routing the sloping, dovetailed sides of the joint in one pass, as shown in the photo on the facing page.

ROBERT TREANOR is a woodworker in San Francisco, Calif.

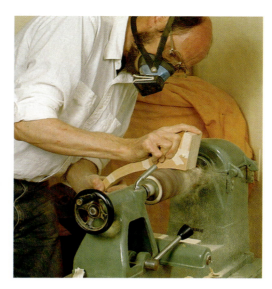

SANDING ALL THE LEGS TO THE SAME SHAPE is easier if the blanks are taped together before sanding to the layout lines. Bandsawing the legs close to the line reduces sanding.

shape of the post is reflected in the profile of the cyma curve, and the thickness of the leg tapers from ¾ in. at the intersection with the post to ½ in. at the tip. Overall, it is a design so clean, so simple, it cannot be improved upon.

As far as I know, there are no measured drawings of this round stand, although pictures and overall dimensions appear in several books. The measured drawing shown on p. 117 is by no means definitive, but it is as close as I have been able to come without actually measuring the original.

Turning the Post

I made this round stand out of clear black cherry, like the original. I turned the post into a 3-in.-dia. cylinder on the lathe, and then I laid out detail lines, as shown in the drawing on p. 117.

Although the turning is fairly straightforward, there are several locations where tolerances are critical. The first is the tenon diameter. I turned the tenon slightly oversized with a parting tool. Then I drilled a hole into a piece of scrap to test the diameter of the tenon. This way, I could turn

SLIDING DOVETAIL PINS ARE CUT EASILY WITH A DOVETAIL BIT in a table-mounted router (above). The author tests the setup with scrap to be sure the pin fits snugly in the socket.

TAPERING THE LEG THICKNESS ON THE JOINTER (above) requires carefully placing the pin end of the leg on the outfeed table and making a single ⅛-in.-deep pass on each side.

the diameter for a perfect match to the drill bit I used to drill the cross brace.

Next, I sized the neck just below the tulip, using the parting tool and caliper. Then I roughed out the shaft, turned the tulip, and undercut the shoulder of the tulip using the tip of a diamond-point tool. With the top of the post completed, I moved the tool rest to the other end and cut the reduced cylinder at the bottom. The actual dimension is not critical, but the cylinder must be perfectly straight to attach the legs properly. The best way to achieve that is with a straight, hardwood block wrapped in sandpaper and used in conjunction with a dial caliper.

Shaping the main shaft is the last step and visually the most difficult. There are only two reference points to rely on, the 1¼ in. dia. at the top and 3 in. dia. at the bottom. A series of light cuts with a sharp gouge got me to the elongated cyma curve that I was after. Then I sanded progressively from 120-grit to 600-grit. Finally, I reversed the rotation of the lathe and then polished the post with #000 steel wool.

Dovetailing the Post

Cutting the dovetail slots for the legs was the next step. Ordinarily, I make one stand at a time and find it just as fast (and a lot more fun) to cut the dovetail slots with a handsaw, chisel, and mallet. But this time, I had two orders of two stands each, plus I needed a stand for display, so I decided to make a cradle to hold the post for cutting the slots with a dovetail bit mounted in my spindle mortiser. An interesting and perhaps more approachable alternative for the home shop is the neat, on-the-lathe, router technique shown in the sidebar on pp. 118–119.

Making the Legs

The legs were cut using the pattern shown in the drawing on p. 117. By tracing the pattern on the stock, I could be sure that the grain ran from the upper corner of the leg to the lower end for the greatest possible strength. For consistency of color, all three legs were cut from the same board. After the legs were bandsawn, I stacked and taped them together with masking tape.

Then I used a disc sander and a pneumatic sanding drum mounted on my lathe to clean up the shape, as shown in the photo on p. 119, sanding one untaped side at a time.

To cut the dovetail pins on the legs (see the left photo on the facing page), I used the same ⅜-in.-dia. dovetail bit I used to cut the slots. Only this time, the bit was in a table-mounted router. I set the depth of cut to the same depth as the dovetailed slot and slid the fence over to cut a dovetail just thicker than the ⅜-in.-dia. bit. Then, through trial-and-error cuts on a piece of scrap, I adjusted the fence until the dovetail pin slid snugly into the slot in the post.

The leg thickness was tapered on the jointer. I set the jointer to ⅛-in. depth of cut and used a wide push stick with a notch to hold the end of the leg. I slowly and carefully placed the upper section of the leg on the outfeed table, as shown in the right photo on the facing page. Then I pushed the leg across the blade, turned it over, and repeated the process on the reverse side.

After completing the other two legs, I belt sanded them to 150 grit and dry-fit them into the post. Using a sharp, pointed knife, I scribed the top of each leg where it joins the post. At the same time, I marked the bottom of the post at the lower edge of the leg. I removed the legs and bandsawed the post to length. Then I sanded the legs to the scribed mark on the pneumatic sanding drum. The top of the legs have the same radius as the post and blended smoothly into the post when reassembled. All legs were then sanded to 600 grit and glued into place.

Completing the Top and Cross Brace

I glued up the top from two pieces cut from a single 10-in.-wide board to match color and grain. While the top was drying, I cut the cross brace, rounded the ends, and drilled the center hole for the post tenon. Then I tapered the rounded ends back

about 2 in. so that only ¼ in. of thickness was left on the ends. Finally, I sanded the brace from 120 grit to 600 grit.

I dry-fit the brace to the tenon, making sure it was perpendicular to one leg. I considered this leg the front of the table and picked the one on the quartersawn side of the post. I made a mark across the tenon, perpendicular to the grain of the brace. With a handsaw, I cut a slot in the tenon and made a wedge to fit. Then I applied glue to the hole in the brace, slid the brace into position, and hammered in the wedge. The post must be hand-held, or the base of the post must be supported on the corner of the bench because the legs won't stand up to these direct hammer blows.

After the tenon was trimmed, I put the base aside to dry while I cut and sanded the top. I bandsawed the top just shy of the layout line and disc sanded to the line. I radiused the top's edge on a slightly deflated pneumatic-drum sander. This could also be done by hand. Although a router would make quick work of shaping the edge, I've never found an appropriate bit with the subtle radius I prefer. I then sanded the edge and both sides of the top to 600 grit.

Before attaching the top, I sanded the bottom of the post flush with the bottom edge of the legs. I lightly chamfered the foot at the bottom of the legs, so they don't splinter and catch on carpeting.

I screwed on the top, centered on the cross brace, and oriented with the brace perpendicular to the grain of the top. The screw holes near the outside edge were elongated to allow for cross-grain movement of the top. The stand was now ready for finishing. The original has a clear varnish finish, but I've used a rubbed-oil finish on mine.

CHRIS BECKSVOORT makes Shaker-style furniture in Maine and is a contributing editor to *Fine Woodworking* magazine.

Although the turning is fairly straightforward, there are several locations where tolerances are critical.

Making an End Table

BY STEPHEN LAMONT

About 10 years ago, I began to tire of my job as a corporate pilot. The work was challenging and enjoyable, but the time away from home put a strain on my family. The job was becoming more technical, too. Temperamentally, I've always been more of a craftsman than a technician.

After considerable soul-searching, I decided to become a furniture maker. I wanted a solid foundation of basic skills, so I went to England, where I trained with Chris Faulkner. He emphasized developing hand-tool skills and building simple, comfortable furniture that asked to be used—a basic tenet of the British Arts-and-Crafts movement. My preferences to this day are for this kind of furniture and for the use of hand tools whenever their use will make a difference.

About two years ago, I designed and built the end table shown in the photo at left. Although it's an original design, many details come from other pieces of furniture in the British Arts-and-Crafts tradition. The joinery is mortise-and-tenon and dovetail throughout.

The construction of the table can be divided into five main steps: stock preparation and panel glue-up; making the front and rear leg assemblies; connecting these two assemblies (including making the shelf and its frame); making and fitting the drawer; and making and attaching the top.

BEAUTY THAT'S MORE THAN SKIN DEEP. This end table is solidly constructed and meticulously detailed. It should last generations.

END TABLE CONSTRUCTION

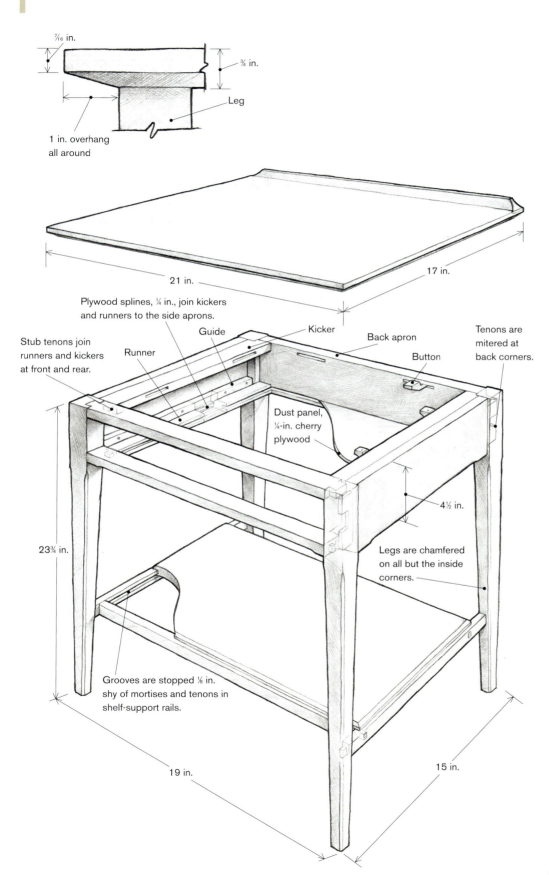

$\frac{7}{16}$ in.

$\frac{3}{4}$ in.

Leg

1 in. overhang all around

21 in.

17 in.

Plywood splines, $\frac{1}{4}$ in., join kickers and runners to the side aprons.

Guide

Kicker

Back apron

Tenons are mitered at back corners.

Stub tenons join runners and kickers at front and rear.

Runner

Button

Dust panel, $\frac{1}{4}$-in. cherry plywood

4½ in.

23¾ in.

Legs are chamfered on all but the inside corners.

Grooves are stopped $\frac{1}{8}$ in. shy of mortises and tenons in shelf-support rails.

19 in.

15 in.

Joinery details

Careful joinery adds to the strength of this Arts-and-Crafts table without compromising its delicate lines.

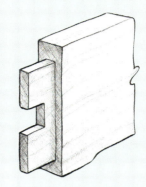

Apron to leg
Two small tenons connected by a stub tenon provide nearly the same glue surface area and resistance to twisting as a full-width tenon, without weakening the leg as much.

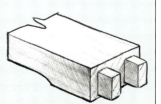

Lower drawer rail to leg
Two small, parallel tenons effectively double the glue surface area that would be available on a single tenon on this delicate frame member.

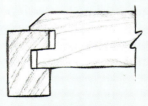

Shelf-to-shelf support rail
The bottom tongue of the shelf's edge nests in the groove of the rail, providing a positive yet inconspicuous connection. The shelf can expand and contract freely with changes in humidity.

KEEPING TRACK OF THE LEGS is easier when they're numbered on top, clockwise from the front left. This system helps prevent layout errors.

MARKING OUT THE DOVETAIL SOCKET. Scribing the socket from the bottom of the slightly tapered dovetail ensures a good fit in the leg.

Stock Selection and Preparation

I milled all the stock for this table to within ¹⁄₁₆ in. of final thickness and width. I also glued up the tabletop, the shelf, and the drawer bottom right away to give them time to move a bit before planing them to final thickness. This helps ensure they'll stay flat in the finished piece. With these three panels in clamps, I dimensioned the rest of the parts to a hair over final thickness. I finish-planed them by hand just before marking out any joinery.

Making the Front and Rear Assemblies

Layout began with the legs. I numbered them clockwise around the perimeter, beginning with the left front as I faced the piece, writing the numbers on the tops of the legs (see the top left photo). This system tells me where each leg goes, which end of a leg is up, and which face is which.

Dovetailing the top rail into the front legs– The dovetails that connect the top rail to the front legs taper slightly top to bottom. I used the narrower bottom of the dovetail to lay out the sockets in the legs. The slight taper ensures a snug fit (see the top right photo). Don't make the dovetails too large, or you'll weaken the legs.

After I marked, cut, and chopped out the sockets, I tested the fit of these dovetails. By using clamping pads and handscrews across the joint, I eliminated the possibility of splitting the leg (see the photo on the facing page). The dovetail should fit snugly but not tightly. Pare the socket, if necessary, until you have a good fit.

Tapering and mortising the legs– I tapered the two inside faces of each leg, beginning 4½ in. down from the top. I removed most of the waste on the jointer and finished the job with a handplane. The tapers must be flat. To avoid planing over a penciled reference line at the top of the taper, I drew hash marks across it. With each stroke of the plane, the lines got shorter. That let me know how close I was getting.

I cut the mortises for this table on a hollow-chisel mortiser. It's quick, and it keeps all the mortises consistent. I made sure all mortises that could be cut with one setting were done at the same time, even if I didn't need the components right away.

Tenoning the aprons and drawer rail—I tenoned the sides, back, and lower drawer rail on the tablesaw, using a double-blade tenoning setup. It takes a little time to get the cut right, but once a test piece fits, tenoning takes just a few minutes. After I cut the tenon cheeks on the tablesaw, I bandsawed just shy of the tenon shoulders and then pared to the line.

One wide apron tenon would have meant a very long mortise, weakening the leg. Instead, I divided the wide tenon into two small tenons separated by a stub tenon (see the drawing detail on p. 123). That left plenty of glue surface area without a big hole in the leg.

Mortising for runners, kickers, and buttons—The drawer rides on runners that are mortised into the lower front rail and the back apron. Similarly, the kickers at the tops of the side aprons, which prevent the drawer from drooping when open, are mortised into the top front rail and the back apron. I cut the ¼-in.-wide mortises for the runner and kicker tenons on the back edge of both drawer rails and on the back apron. There are eight mortises for the drawer runners and kickers. Another seven mortises of the same size are for the buttons that attach the top to the table's base—three on the back apron and two on each kicker.

I also cut grooves for the dust panel at this time. The ¼-in.-thick panel is set into the frame of the table just below the drawer. It's a nice touch, even if it's not needed structurally. I cut the grooves for the panel into the bottom of the back apron and into the back of the drawer rail. (I cut the dust-panel grooves in the drawer runners later.) Then I made a test-fit with a scrap of the same ¼-in. cherry plywood used for the panel.

CHECKING THE FIT OF THE TOP-RAIL DOVETAIL. A handscrew prevents a leg from splitting if the dovetail is too big. The fit should be snug but not tight.

Carving a Lamb's Tongue

STEP 1
PARE TO MARKED BASE-LINE. Strive for a fair, even curve and cut down toward the chamfer.

STEP 2
TAP A STOP FOR THE SHOULDER AT THE BASE-LINE. Avoid cutting too deeply; just a light tap is needed.

STEP 3
PARE INTO STOP TO CREATE A SHOULDER. You have to cut toward the shoulder, so take light cuts and watch which way the grain is running. If you must pare against the grain, make sure your chisel is freshly honed.

Chamfering and gluing up–Stopped chamfers are routed on the legs and aprons of this table, each terminating in a carved lamb's tongue. I stopped routing just shy of the area to be carved and then carved the tongue and the little shoulder in three steps, as shown in the photos at left.

Gluing up the table base is a two-step process. First, I connected the front legs with the top and bottom drawer rails and the back legs with the back apron. To prevent the legs from toeing in or out because of clamping pressure, I inserted spacers between the legs at their feet and clamped both the top and bottom. Then I checked for square, measuring diagonally from corner to corner (see the photo on the facing page). It ensures that the assembly is square and that the legs are properly spaced.

Connecting the Front and Rear Assemblies

To hold the legs in position while I measured for the drawer runners and kickers and, later, to get the spacing on shelf-support rails correct, I made a simple frame of hardboard and wooden corner blocks (see the photo on p. 128). The frame ensures the assembly is square and the legs are properly spaced. After I marked the shoulder-to-shoulder lengths for the runners and kickers, I cut and fit the stub tenons that join these pieces to the front and rear assemblies. The back ends of the runners and kickers must be notched to fit around the inside corners of the legs.

Runners, kickers, and dust panel–I cut the ¼-in. grooves for the dust panel in the drawer runners next. I also cut grooves for the splines with which I connected the drawer runners and kickers to the sides of the table. There are 10 grooves in all—one each on the inside and outside edges of the drawer runners, one on the outside edge of each of the kickers, and two in each side for the splines.

CHECK DIAGONALS TO MAKE SURE ASSEMBLIES ARE GLUED UP SQUARE. **Clamps and a spacer at the bottom of the legs prevent the clamping pressure at the top from causing the legs to toe in or out.**

Then I dry-clamped the table and made sure the tops of the kickers were flush with the top edges of the sides, the tops of the runners flush with the top of the drawer rail, and the bottoms of the runners flush with the bottom edges of the sides. Then I cut the dust panel to size, test-fit it, and set it aside until glue-up.

Building the shelf frame and shelf—The shelf on this table is a floating panel captured by a frame made of four rails. The two rails that run front to back are tenoned into the legs; the other two are joined to the first pair with through-wedged tenons.

I put the dry-assembled table into the hardboard frame and clamped the legs to the blocks. Then I clamped the pair of rails that will be tenoned into the legs against the inside surfaces of the legs and marked the shoulder of each tenon (see the photo on p. 128). I also marked the rails for

orientation so that the shoulders can be mated correctly with the legs.

Tenons were cut and fit next. With the rails dry-clamped into the legs, I measured for the two remaining rails to be joined to the first pair. I laid out and cut the through-mortises in the first set of rails, chopping halfway in from each side to prevent tearout. I cut the tenons on the second set of rails, assembled the frame and marked the through-tenons with a pencil line for wedge orientation. So they don't split the rails, the wedges must be perpendicular to the grain of the mortised rail.

I flared the sides of the through-mortises (not the tops and bottoms) so the outside of the mortise is about ⅙ in. wider than the inside. This taper, which goes about three-quarters of the way into the mortise, lets the wedges splay the tenon, locking the rail into the mortise like a dovetail.

Next, I marked the location of the wedge kerfs in each tenon, scribing a line from both sides of the tenon with a mark-ing gauge for uniformity. I cut the kerfs at a slight angle. Wedges must fill both the kerf and the gap in the widened mortise, so they need to be just over ⅙ in. thick at their widest.

An interlocking tongue and groove connects the shelf to the rails that support it (see the drawing detail on p. 123). Using a ¼-in. slot cutter in my table-mounted router, I cut the groove in the rails, working out the fit on test pieces first. The slots are ¼ in. deep. I stopped the grooves in the rails ⅛ in. or so short of the mortises on the side rails and short of the tenon shoulders on the front and back rails. I notched the shelf to fit at the corners (see the drawing on p. 123).

I measured the space between the rails of the shelf frame and added ½ in. in each direction to get the shelf dimensions. I cut the tongue on all four edges on the router table.

Gluing up the shelf-frame assembly–
Before gluing up the shelf frame, I routed hollows in clamp pads to fit over the through-tenons on two of the shelf rails. Then I began gluing up the shelf assembly. I applied glue sparingly in the mortises and on the tenons so I wouldn't accidentally glue the shelf in place. I pulled the joints tight with clamps and then removed the clamps temporarily so I could insert the wedges.

After tapping the lightly glue-coated wedges into the kerfs in the tenons, I reclamped the frame. I checked diagonals and adjusted the clamps until the assembly was square. Once the glue was dry, I sawed off the protruding tenons and wedges and planed them flush.

Overall glue-up–With the shelf frame glued up, the entire table was ready to be assembled. I began the large front-to-back glue-up by dry-clamping the front and back leg assemblies, sides, runners, kickers (with splines), dust panel, and shelf assembly. I made adjustments and then glued up.

I made and fit the drawer guides next (see the drawing on p. 123 for placement). I glued the guides to both the sides and the runners and screwed them to the sides with deeply countersunk brass screws.

I did a thorough cleanup of the table in preparation for drawer fitting. I removed remaining glue, ironed out dents, and sanded the entire piece with 120-grit sandpaper on a block. I gently pared sharp corners, taking care not to lose overall crispness.

The Drawer

I particularly enjoy making and fitting drawers. A well-made drawer that whispers in and out gives me great satisfaction. I use the traditional British system of drawermaking, which produces what my teachers called a piston fit. The process is painstaking, but the results are well worth the effort. That, however, is a story for another day.

Making and Attaching the Top

After I thicknessed and cut the top to size, I placed it face down on my bench. I set the glued-up base upside down on the top and oriented it so it would have a 1-in. overhang all around. I marked the positions of the outside corners and connected them with a pencil line around the perimeter. This line is one edge of the bevel on the underside of the top. Then I used a marking gauge to strike a line ⁷⁄₁₆ in. from the top surface on all four edges. Connecting the two lines at the edges created the bevel angle (see the drawing on p. 123). I roughed out the bevel on the tablesaw and cleaned it up with a plane. The bevels should appear to grow out of the tops of the legs.

Making and attaching the coved lip–The cove at the back of the top is a strip set into a rabbet at the back. I cut the cove from the same board I used for the top so that grain and color would match closely. I ripped the cove strip on the tablesaw and handplaned it to fit the rabbet. I shaped the strip on the router table, leaving the point at which it

RABBETED CLAMPING BLOCK HELPS PROVIDE PRESSURE IN TWO PLANES. The author clamps down the cove strip with six C-clamps and into the rabbet with six bar clamps. A spring clamp on each end closes any visible gaps at the ends.

intersects the top slightly proud. To provide even clamping pressure, I used a rabbeted caul, clamping both down and in (see the photo at left).

When the glue was dry, I planed the back and the ends of the cove flush with the top. To form a smooth transition between top and cove in front, I used a curved scraper, followed by sandpaper on a block shaped to fit the cove. I frequently checked the transition with my hand and sanded a wider swath toward the end. It's easy to go too far and have a nasty dip in front of the cove.

I drew the ends of the cove with a French curve and then shaped the ends with a coping saw, chisel, and sandpaper. The curve should blend into the tabletop seamlessly.

Finishing up with oil—After finish sanding, I applied several coats of raw linseed oil diluted with mineral spirits in a 50/50 mix, a few more coats of straight linseed oil, and, finally, two to three coats of tung oil to harden the surface. I let the oil dry thoroughly between coats. After the last coat of oil was dry, I rubbed the surface down with a Scotch-Brite pad and gave the table a few coats of paste wax. The drawer was the exception: Aside from the face of the drawer front, all other surfaces were finished with wax alone.

Attaching the top—I screwed the top to the top-drawer rail from beneath to fix its position at the front. That way, the mating of the bevel with the front rail will be correct and any seasonal movement of the top will be at the back. I attached the top to the base with buttons on the sides and in the rear.

STEPHEN LAMONT is a professional furniture maker. He recently accepted a position as craftsman with the Edward Barnsley Educational Trust in Hampshire, England.

A Sturdy Footstool

BY MARIO RODRIGUEZ

That top shelf is always just inches out of your reach. If you were a couple of inches taller, you would not have to trudge to the garage for that shaky, paint-spattered stepladder. At a time like this, wouldn't a neat little footstool be the perfect answer, tall enough to give the needed boost but small enough to tuck underneath a desk or in a corner? Small stools are also a favorite with kids, helping them do things on their own, from sneaking cookies to brushing teeth.

Recently I built this sturdy stool in mahogany. This simple project is a perfect way to spend a woodworking weekend. It can be made of short scrap pieces or a single board 10 in. wide by 50 in. long. It has just four parts (two of them identical), and only one type of joint to practice and perfect. It's a manageable project for a novice, but the angled through-tenons will offer a challenge to any level of woodworker.

The height of the stool is about 9 in., a little taller than a typical stair tread, keeping it compact. Yet the step is large enough to

SIMPLE JIGS ensure that angled joints come together without a hitch.

FULL-SIZED DRAWINGS ANSWER QUESTIONS

The legs are tapered and canted to angle outward on all sides. The resulting footprint determines the dimensions of the top. Make an accurate full-sized drawing to guide the construction of this project. It will be easier to take dimensions and angles directly from your drawing than to work them out mathematically. Note: The mortises are a heavy ¾ in. square to allow a standard chisel to slide in easily.

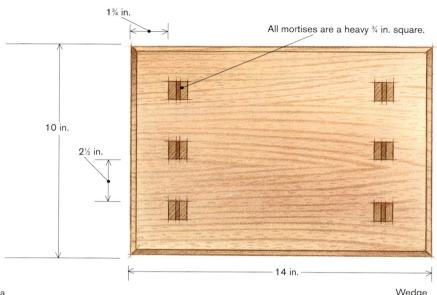

1¾ in.

All mortises are a heavy ¾ in. square.

10 in.

2½ in.

14 in.

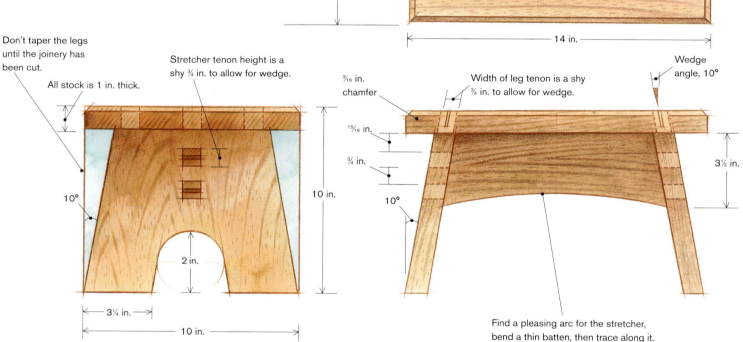

Don't taper the legs until the joinery has been cut.

All stock is 1 in. thick.

Stretcher tenon height is a shy ¾ in. to allow for wedge.

10°

2 in.

3¼ in.

10 in.

10 in.

³⁄₁₆ in. chamfer

Width of leg tenon is a shy ¾ in. to allow for wedge.

Wedge angle, 10°

¹⁵⁄₁₆ in.

¾ in.

10°

3½ in.

Find a pleasing arc for the stretcher, bend a thin batten, then trace along it.

easily accommodate two adult feet, side by side, with the splayed legs adding stability.

As with the dovetail, I find the through-mortise-and-tenon joint irresistible. I like the strong contrasting squares of end grain that break up the wood's surface. But this joint invites close inspection, so make it tight and clean. Unlike a single mortise and tenon, where a misfit can be fudged ¹⁄₁₆ in. one way or another, this joint must be dead-on. Wedging the tenons fills gaps, but only in one direction. Making the joinery more complicated is the 10° cant of the

legs. However, I've come up with some jigs and techniques that will make things much easier on you.

Success Starts on Paper

I began this project by making a full-sized drawing. By laying the pieces on the drawing as you proceed, you can check the dimensions and angles of each part and the position of the mortises.

After thicknessing the mahogany stock, rip the pieces to width, and cut them to length. Leave an extra ¹⁄₁₆ in. of length for leveling the legs and trimming the through-tenons later.

Leg-to-Top Joinery

The key to cutting these joints successfully is to lay out everything very carefully. Working from the drawing, mark out the thickness of the mortises across the top. Go ¹⁄₁₆ in. more than the thickness of the leg tenons. This will leave a gap for the wedging action to come later.

For the horizontal layout of the mortises —which must be dead-on—use a layout gauge, which is a small story stick that will standardize the width and spacing of mortises and tenons. Transfer marks from your full-sized drawing onto a small stick; then use the stick to mark all of the mortises in the top and the tenons on the legs. For a clean outline, I use a sharp marking knife. Each mortise is a little larger than ¾ in. to allow a ¾-in. chisel to slip in easily.

Accurate angled mortises–These mortises and tenons aren't straight up; they're angled at 10°. The key to a great fit is to ensure that the mortises are sloped very precisely, so the exposed tenon completely fills the mortise without any gaps. However, we'll work from the top side of the workpiece, where the accuracy of the mortise and tenon will be most evident, toward the bottom side, where the ⅛-in. shoulders around the tenon will hide small gaps. So relax— a little.

Drill out the majority of the waste on a drill press–supporting the workpiece with a 10° ramp and using a ¾-in. Forstner bit (see the photo and drawing on p.134). This makes the chisel work much easier. The other secret to cutting these mortises accurately is to use a chisel guide (see the photos and drawings on p.135). This is a simple jig made of three faces, each one cut to 10°. The center section, which matches the

MARK THE OUTLINES AND SPACING OF THE MORTISES IN THE TOP. With two lines already scribed to mark the thickness of the mortises, use the layout gauge to mark the other edges.

fat ¾-in. width of the mortises, is set back about 1 in. This pocket keeps the back of the chisel at the 10° angle and regulates the width of the mortise. The two angled sections that jut forward are used as a visual guide to keep the back of the chisel at the same angle when you work on the opposite angled wall of the mortise.

I square up the drilled holes with a series of chisels. I use a ¼-in. chisel to cut corners into the round holes and create a little room, then turn to my ½-in. mortise chisel to ride the slope and sides of the guide block and cut the mortise to shape. Finally, I use a ¾-in. chisel to clean up the walls, flaring them slightly toward the hidden (bottom) side of the mortise, to allow easier assembly without compromising the appearance of the completed joint. Be sure to back up your workpiece with a piece of scrap to prevent blowing out the back of the mortise where your chisel exits.

While you're set up to drill and square up the mortises, do the pair of mortises in each of the legs. Use the plywood ramp and the chisel guide again—but pay close

PLYWOOD RAMP

Make this simple jig with plywood and drywall screws. Adjust the riser block until the slope of the jig reads 10° on a large protractor.

Slope, 10°

DRILL OUT THE ANGLED MORTISES. Use the ramp to position the workpiece at 10°. Square the workpiece with the edge of the ramp to be sure that the drilling angle is aligned properly. Then drill the mortises with a ¾-in. Forstner bit.

attention to the direction of the angle in relation to the mortises. You don't need a layout stick here, because the extra room for wedging adds a fudge factor to the spacing of these double mortises and tenons. As you proceed, check everything against your full-sized drawing.

The leg tenons–The next step in joining the legs to the top is to lay out and cut the leg tenons. Remember to leave them a little

long, to be trimmed flush later. While the legs are still square (the sides untapered), cut the ⅛-in.-wide shoulders to their 10° angle on the tablesaw, working by eye to a layout line. After returning the sawblade to 90°, stand the board on end and cut the outside cheeks.

Next mark out the width and position of each tenon using the layout gauge, and make the interior cheek cuts on the bandsaw. Use the 10° plywood ramp to make

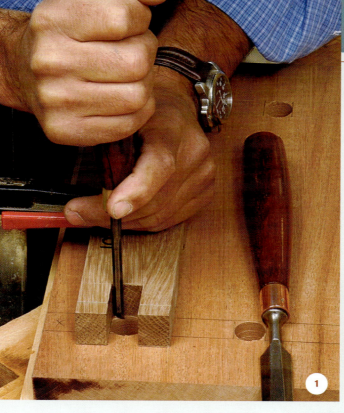

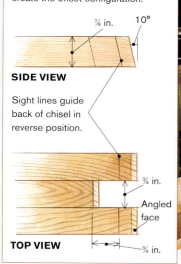
Use the sight line to keep the chisel at the correct angle.

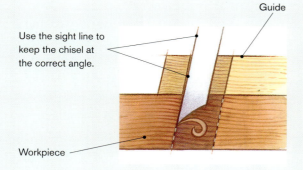

Guide

Workpiece

THREE-CHISEL PROCESS. With the help of the chisel guide, use a ¼-in. chisel to remove the corners (1), a ½-in. mortising chisel to rough out the rest (2), and a ¾-in. chisel to clean up the walls (3).

GUIDE WORKS BOTH WAYS. The chisel guide also helps you cut the opposite angled wall of the mortise. Draw a line on the wall of the chisel guide parallel to its front edge.

the bandsaw blade meet the tenon shoulders evenly.

Cut out the waste with a coping saw, then use a chisel to trim the shoulders and pare the cheeks. Monitor your progress by frequently placing the top over the leg tenons and looking down into the mortises to see how the tenons are lining up.

As you continue to test-fit the pieces, note that the tenons should fit snugly across their width, but there should be wedging room left in their thickness.

Add the Stretcher Next

Working from your drawing, lay out the stretcher. Cut the ends on the chopsaw to 10°. You've already cut the mortises in the legs. Now you can cut the stretcher tenons using the same techniques and jigs as before; however, note that the stretcher tenons are angled in a different direction from the

Tenons

SET THE BLADE TO 90° TO CUT THE OUTSIDE CHEEKS. This board is wide enough to be run on end. There will be a little waste left to be pared away later. The opposite cheek will require a change in blade height.

CUT THE ANGLED SHOULDERS. Set the tablesaw blade angle to 10° and work to a scribed layout line when cutting the narrow outside shoulders.

THIS SIMPLE FOOT-STOOL, which can be made from scrap, is a useful project that can be built in a weekend.

leg-to-top joinery. Once again, there is extra space in the mortise for the wedging action. Start on the tablesaw, cutting the outside shoulders and cheeks of the tenons. But before moving on, set the legs into the top and place the stretcher shoulders between them to check the fit.

When you are done cutting and fitting the tenons, bandsaw the curve along the underside. Again, you can clean up the curve with a spindle sander or with a spokeshave and cabinet scraper, as I do.

The Leg Taper and Cutout

The sides of the legs also have a 10° ta-per. Take the angle and dimensions off the full-sized drawing and cut just off the line on the bandsaw. Then smooth the edges on the jointer or with a handplane.

Beside adding a little visual interest to the design, the leg cutout helps to over-come an uneven floor. Draw the arc with a

  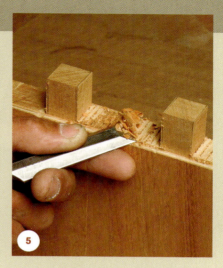

USE THE SAME LAYOUT GAUGE FOR THE TENONS. There is no room for error here, and the layout gauge will ensure that the tenons match the mortises.

USE THE ANGLED RAMP ON THE BANDSAW. This lets the blade cut all the way to the angled shoulder. Leave a little on the cheeks for paring, and cut kerfs into the waste areas.

FIT THE LEG TO THE TOP. Clean up the shoulders with a sharp chisel, then pare the sides of the tenons, checking them frequently against their mating mortises.

compass, and use a sliding bevel to extend the lines parallel to the taper of the legs. Again, make the rough cut on the bandsaw, and then clean up the cutout with a spindle sander or with rasps, files, and sandpaper, as I do.

Assembly is Also Tricky

This is a difficult project to assemble because all of the parts—and all of the mortises and tenons—must converge at once. First you should assemble different parts, placing the partial assemblies on the drawing and against each other to check angles and fit. After tweaking and adjusting the parts, dry-fit the whole stool.

Getting the stool together and apart again won't be easy. Some advice: Work carefully, move slowly, and be patient. Then position your clamps and slowly draw the stool together. Listen for creaks and groans, and watch for splits. If you see the leading edge of the tenon splitting the top edge of a mortise upward, either tap the split area down with a mallet and small block, or trim the tenon.

Kerf the tenons for the wedges—Before gluing up, saw a thin kerf into the end of each tenon. This kerf will receive a small wedge, which will spread apart the tenon, locking it in place and closing the small gap. I find that a handsaw makes an appropriate kerf. Go about ¾ in. deep. Note that the wedges in through-tenons should always be oriented against the grain surrounding the mortise; otherwise, the wedges, which pack a lot of punch, will split the mortised piece.

After applying white glue, which sets more slowly than yellow, draw all of the parts together completely. Let things set up for roughly 15 minutes, remove the clamps and blocks, and tap in the wedges with a little glue on the tip of each one. A good

THE PARTS ALL CONVERGE AT ONCE DURING GLUE-UP. Dry-fit everything beforehand. Assemble one leg and the top, the other leg and the stretcher, then drive the joints together carefully.

WALNUT WEDGES ADD CONTRAST. Cut the wedges to a 10° angle and tap them into the kerfs in the tenons until the tenons spread to fill the mortises.

angle for these small wedges is 10°. Tap them in until the gap around the tenon closes.

Finishing Up

Leave the stool for at least 12 hours to let the wedges set up firmly. Then trim and plane them flush.

The last detail before sanding and finishing the piece is to chamfer the top. First, scribe lines ³⁄₁₆ in. back from the edge. Then, with a block plane angled at 45°, work down to the lines to leave a crisp, even chamfer. Of course, a router would also do the job, but I like the subtle character of handwork.

MARIO RODRIGUEZ is a contributing editor to *Fine Woodworking* magazine. He teaches woodworking in the furniture-restoration program at the Fashion Institute of Technology in New York City.

Oval Chippendale Stool

It's real easy to get excited about making a stool like this. Compressed into this little gem are the chief hallmarks of the Colonial Philadelphia chairmakers: finely carved feet on graceful legs tenoned into a thin curved frame, topped off with an upholstered slip seat. Less than a handful of original oval stools exist today. To my eye, this Chippendale-style stool commands a presence far beyond the small amount of material needed to build it.

With its curves, carving, and fine proportions, 18th-century-style furniture is hard to ignore. Over the years, I've built all kinds of things from wood, but making furniture in this style continues to offer the most satisfying challenge. That challenge lies not just in the cutting and carving but in researching the history and construction details of the piece.

In my part of the country, there are not a lot of original examples of this type of furniture to examine, so to capture the essence of a particular piece, I have to do a lot of homework. First, I read all of the related books and magazine articles I can find. Then I travel to check out similar pieces in museums or, if possible, in private collections. The research is far more time-consuming than actually making the piece.

This stool is an outstanding example of the Philadelphia Chippendale school of chairmaking. For chairs with curved seats, Colonial Philadelphia chairmakers tenoned the legs up into a stout frame. In most other areas, chairmakers tenoned the frame members into the leg the same way a table's aprons are tenoned into its legs; that resulted in a strong joint but a wide frame. The Philadelphia approach sacrificed just a little bit of strength for an elegantly thin frame.

BY RANDALL O'DONNELL

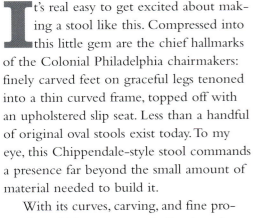

THE CURVED FRAME and the carved cabriole legs come together.

MASSIVE TIMBERS AND SIMPLE JOINERY

This handsome little stool starts as a hefty rectangular frame.

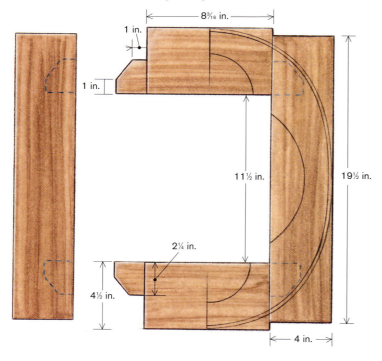

ASSEMBLE THE FRAME. The bulk of the frame has been reduced by bandsawing arc-shaped segments prior to assembly.

Although making a curved frame and attaching curved legs may appear daunting, the joinery is dirt simple. In this chapter, I'll describe how to construct the frame and make and carve the legs. I'll also show you a foolproof assembly process and touch on applying the finish.

Make Full-sized Patterns and a Rabbeting Template

Start by making full-sized plywood patterns of the seat frame, leg, and knee block (for dimensions, see the drawings above and on the facing page). Additionally, you'll need to make a template to guide the router for wasting away material to form the rabbet for the slip seat.

The frame pattern provides the curve of the oval and the mortise location for the leg tenon. To avoid cutting errors, enlarge this quarter-segment pattern to full size and use it to make a complete oval pattern. Mark out one quarter of the oval and then, using the centerlines as reference marks, flip

A ROUTER MAKES FAST WORK OF THE SEAT RABBET. Use a full-sized oval pattern to establish the layout line.

THIS GOUGE IS GOOD. To hog away stock the router couldn't reach, the author used a gouge.

OVAL CHIPPENDALE STOOL

Full-sized patterns help avoid errors and simplify layout. These patterns are 40-percent scale.
Use a copying machine to enlarge them to full size or use the grid to develop the full-sized patterns.

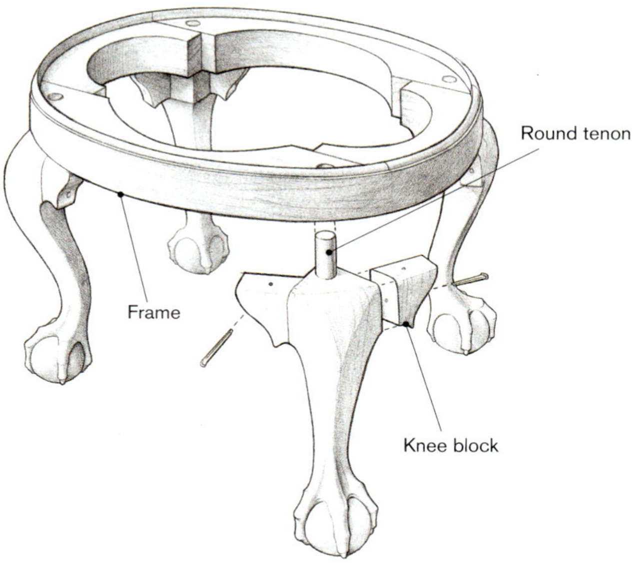

2¾ in.

2¾ in.

⅝ in.

⅝ in.

⅞ in. dia.

Round tenon

Frame

Knee block

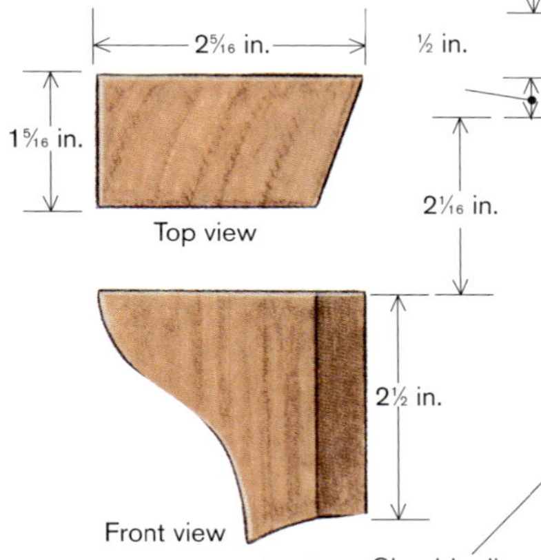

2⁵⁄₁₆ in.

½ in.

1⁵⁄₁₆ in.

2¹⁄₁₆ in.

Top view

2½ in.

Front view

Knee Block

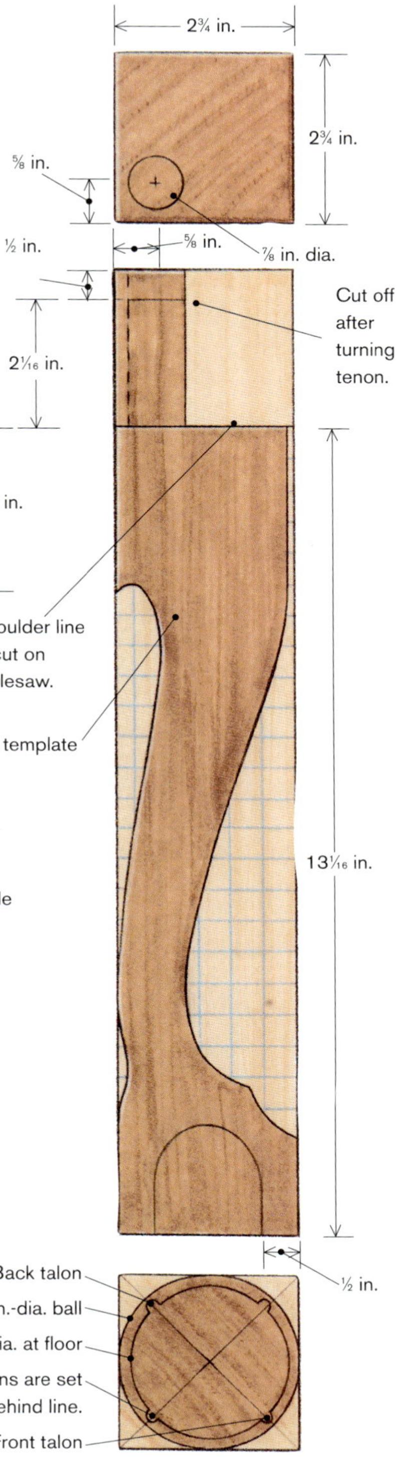

Shoulder line
is cut on
tablesaw.

Cut off
after
turning
tenon.

Leg template

13¹⁄₁₆ in.

⅛ in. dia.

1¼ in.

1⅛ in.

Tendon

Knuckle

Web

Ball

Talon

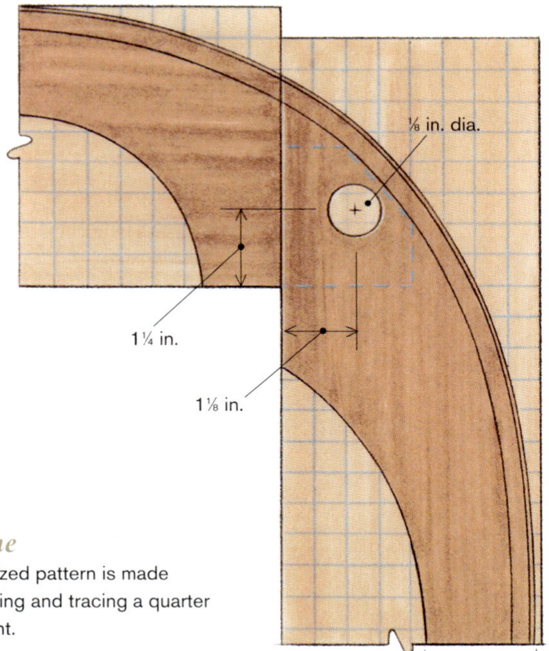

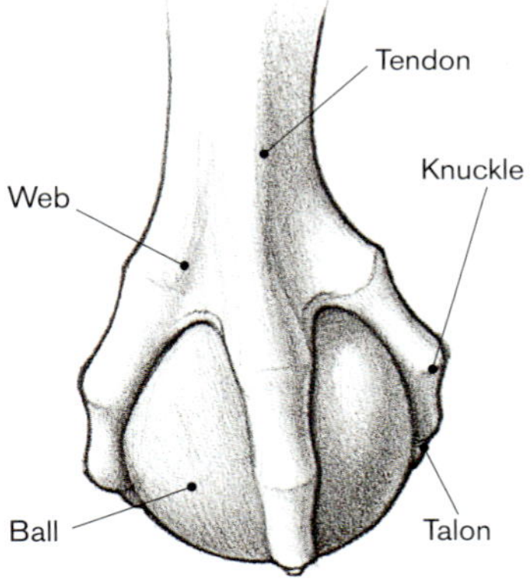

Ball-and-Claw Foot

Frame

A full-sized pattern is made
by flipping and tracing a quarter
segment.

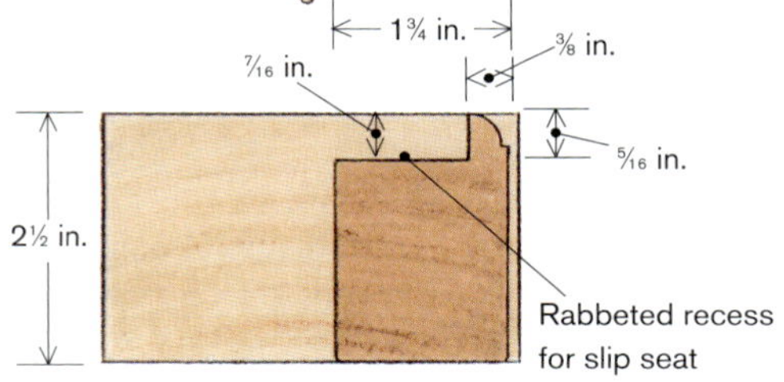

1¾ in.

³⁄₈ in.

⁷⁄₁₆ in.

⁵⁄₁₆ in.

2½ in.

Rabbeted recess
for slip seat

Stock is oriented with
heart side down.

Back talon

2¾-in.-dia. ball

2⁷⁄₁₆ in. dia. at floor

Side talons are set
slightly behind line.

Front talon

½ in.

Leg

Carving a Ball-and-Claw Foot

1. ESTABLISH A CYLINDER

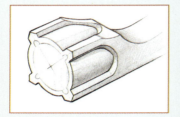

OUTLINE THE TOES WITH A V-PARTING TOOL. Cut to the depth of the larger circle marked on the bottom of the foot.

SHAPE BETWEEN THE TOES. Use a #2 gouge and cut to a cylindrical form between the toes.

2. SHAPE THE BALL

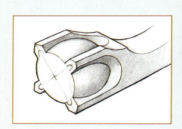

ROUND THE TOP, THEN THE BOTTOM. Carve from the equator toward the ankle with a #2 gouge. Work around the ball to develop a sphere. Then carve down from the equator to shape the bottom of the ball.

3. LOCATE AND CARVE THE KNUCKLES

MARK THE KNUCKLES. The front and side toes have three knuckles; the back toe has two.

SHAPE THE TOES. Round over and slightly undercut the toes. The areas between the knuckles are scalloped and thinner than the joints.

4. CUT THE TALONS AND TENONS

CARVE THE TALONS. Taper the talons to about ⅛ in. at the bottom of the foot. Note that the side talons taper to a point slightly behind the line.

PROMINENT TENDONS PRODUCE A STRONG-LOOKING GRIP. Define the tendons and web using a #8 bent gouge. Work up from the ball to the knee.

FOUR-LEGGED UNIFORMITY. Complete each stage on all legs before moving on to the next stage. Use rifflers and sandpaper for a refined foot.

LIGHTEN THE LOAD, THEN TURN THE TENON. Rough bandsaw the leg, leaving a bridge of material to hold the first cutoff in place. When turning the tenon, use a short tool rest for best support.

build the frame, start by milling the stock to 2½ in. thick and cutting the four frame members to size. It helps to orient the frame stock so that the heart side faces down. This orientation results in an arc-shaped grain pattern that rises toward the middle of the frame, which looks much better than a slumping grain pattern.

Referring to the full-sized pattern, mark out and cut the mortises and tenons. For mortising, I use a plunge router to remove most of the waste and hand-chisel the corners and sloping transition in the mortise. A bandsaw makes fast work of the tenons. Again, I carefully pare to the layout line with a chisel.

Many original Philadelphia pieces simply left the inside of the beefy frame rectangular, but I prefer to cut away a lot of the excess bulk to reduce the mass. Prior to assembly, I bandsaw large arc-shaped hunks from the frame interior.

Now, glue up the frame. Don't worry about clamp marks on the frame edges, because they will be cut away when you saw the oval. After the glue dries, use the pattern to mark out the ⅞-in.-dia. mortises and then drill them.

Some Philadelphia chairmakers used a separate, applied lip to house the slip seat because it was more economical. For me, it's easier to make the lip by rabbeting the frame, using a router to waste away the excess stock quickly. Using an exterior template and router guide bushing prevents cutting into the lip. Because the router base is too small to provide adequate support while cutting the area toward the middle of the frame, I use a gouge to pare away the waste. After rabbeting the frame, saw it to the oval shape on the bandsaw. I use an oscillating edge belt sander to clean up the profile to the scribe line.

An edge bead on the seat rim forms a neat transition from the frame to the slip seat. The rabbeting template offcut, placed where the slip seat goes, provides the plat-

the pattern over to mark out the remaining quadrants.

I make a plywood router template for rabbeting the frame for the slip seat. When sizing the oval opening in the template, figure in the offset between the router bit and the guide bushing you will use to cut the rabbet. Be sure to save the interior offcut from the rabbeting jig. It will be used as a router platform for cutting the bead on the top edge of the frame.

Join a Rectangular Frame, then Shape the Oval

It's astonishing that this small stool starts out with timber-frame-sized members. To

TEMPORARY FIXING. With the ball and claw complete, prepare to carve the knee by dry-fitting the leg to the frame. Use screws through the knee blocks to hold the leg in place.

form for supporting the router. You could use a standard beading bit for this edge bead, but I prefer to end up with a less-machined-looking result.

I first make a 1/16-in. rabbet around perimeter of the frame and then round over the top edge with a cabinetmaker's file. Develop the bead by making a series of small parallel chamfers, with the grain, along the perimeter of the frame. I think the slight irregularities resulting from this process give an authentic handworked look to the piece.

Bandsaw the Cabriole Legs, then Turn the Tenon

The leg material should be sound, straight-grained stock. Cut the 2¾-in. square leg billets to size. Allow an extra ½ in. of length on the tenon end for the lathe's spur center. It will be cut off after the tenon has been turned. Use a full-sized pattern to mark out two faces of each leg. Orient the pattern on the leg billet so that the resulting leg pro-

files are knee to knee. Mark the center point of the round tenon on both ends. To define the start of the tenon, cut the shoulder lines at the top of the knee on the tablesaw.

Before turning the leg, cut the cabriole shape on the bandsaw to reduce the leg mass and lathe vibration during the tenon turning. When cutting cabriole legs, I use the bridge method to eliminate the need for reattaching the offcut stock. Briefly, when bandsawing the first cabriole profile, don't saw off the waste completely. Instead, leave a small bridge between the leg and the waste. This allows you to cut the other side of the leg profile without having to re-attach the sawn-away stock. Cut through the bridge after the second profile has been cut.

Once the leg has been rough-cut, turn the tenon. Mount the leg on the lathe with the tenon nearest the headstock. The spinning blur of a leg may look a little scary, but it's quite safe because all of the work is

The Philadelphia approach sacrificed just a bit of strength for an elegantly thin frame.

confined to the tenon. Use a short tool rest so there's no chance of getting pinched between the leg and the tool rest.

Carve the Feet

By about 1755, the ball-and-claw foot had become firmly identified with the American Chippendale style. The motif is thought to have originated in China as a dragon's claw clutching a pearl. To make the feet for this stool, draw two concentric circles on the bottom of each foot. A 2¾-in.-dia. circle is the full diameter of the ball. A 2⁷⁄₁₆-in.-dia. circle is the ball diameter at the floor. Mark the equator—the horizontal center-line of the ball—⅝ in. from the bottom of each foot. Now, mark the toe outline from the drawing.

To achieve uniformity, carve the four legs together, advancing all four from one stage to the next. I use only a few carving tools to make the feet: a V-parting tool, a #2 gouge, a #8 long-bent or #8 spoon gouge, a rasp, and a riffler. The tool numbers refer to the gouge's cutting-edge radius, or sweep.

Start by outlining the toes on the ball using a V-parting tool. Using the #2 gouge and the V-parting tool to refine the outline, cut the ball area to a cylinder by working to the layout line marked on the bottom of the foot. Then smooth this area with a rasp to produce a nice, uniform surface. With the #2 gouge, round the top area of the ball, working from the equator and deepening the toe-to-ball junction with the V-parting tool. Be careful not to remove any stock from the center point of the equator—this is the basic reference for the ball diameter. Round the lower half of the ball, working down to the inner circle. Keep referring to the other three surfaces between the toes to maintain the spherical shape. Once you have the ball rounded, smooth it with a riffler.

Now, mark out the toe joints: three on the front toes and two on the back. Round over the toes, slightly undercutting them at the ball surface. Scallop and thin the toes between the knuckles, making the knuckles more prominent. Once the toes have been

defined and rounded, mark out the talons ½ in. from the bottom of the foot—Philadelphia-style ball-and-claw feet tend to have rather stubby talons. Note that even though the side toes are forward at the centerline for most of their length, their talons taper to a point slightly behind the centerline. The front and back talons are aligned on the centerline. Taper the talons to about ⅛ in. dia.

Now comes the part that really gives a feeling of tension in the foot: cutting the web and defining the tendons. Use a #8

GLUE THE LEGS IN THE FRAME. The knee blocks temporarily screwed to the frame ensure that the legs go back in the same position. The knee blocks are glued in place after the leg glue joint has started to set.

long-bent gouge and start defining the extent of the tendons. Work from the ball up toward the knee, leaving the web proud of the ball by about 1/16 in. Smooth the carving with rifflers and small pieces of sandpaper. Shape the leg from the ankle to the knee with a rasp and rough-sand the lower leg and foot. The upper leg will be shaped and faired to the frame in the next step.

Fit the Knee Blocks and Fair the Upper Legs

The knee blocks make the visual transition from the legs to the frame and buttress the joint. Fitting knee blocks to a curved frame is somewhat different from the usual rectangular frame because the blocks flare away from the leg to meet the frame.

Dry-fit the legs into the frame, aligning the flat knee-block surface of the leg parallel to the frame's joint line. Now, screw the knee blocks in place to hold the leg in this position for rough shaping the upper leg. Be sure to mark the legs and knee blocks so that you can return them to the same positions on the frame. Carefully remove the legs without disturbing the knee blocks.

Finish up

With the knee blocks still screwed in place, glue the legs to the frame. Once the glue has started to set (about 10 minutes), remove the knee blocks, one at a time, apply glue, and screw them back in place. After the glue-up, replace the screws in the knee blocks with hand-forged nails for authenticity.

After the glue dries, use a #2 gouge and a patternmaker's rasp to blend the curves of the upper legs and knee blocks into the frame. The final smoothing is done with sandpaper, starting at 100 grit and ending with 180 grit. Sponge with water, then give the surfaces a quick hit with 400-grit paper to remove any raised wood fibers.

Susy, my patient wife, does the finishing and really gets the wood's figure to pop. She colors the wood with red mahogany aniline dye, followed by a washcoat of shellac. Two separate applications of paste filler with a black tint, spaced a day apart, follow. Finally, several coats of buttonlac shellac topped off with Behlen's violin varnish make the stool glow.

Crowning this regal little stool with a silk damask-covered slip seat completes the project. I make the frame, and an upholsterer does the webbing, padding, and fitting of the fabric. To make the frame, I simply join a rectangular assembly of poplar, bandsaw it to the oval shape 1/8 in. smaller all around than the seat recess, and cut a heavy chamfer around the top outside edge.

RANDALL O'DONNELL makes period-style furniture at his shop in the countryside near Bloomington, Ind.

The articles in this book appeared in the following issues of *Fine Woodworking*:

p. 4: A Small Elegant Box by Gary Rogowski, issue 139. Photos by Matthew Teague, courtesy *Fine Woodworking*, © The Taunton Press, Inc.; Drawings courtesy *Fine Woodworking*, © The Taunton Press, Inc.

p. 10: Making Mitered Boxes by Gary Rogowski, issue 162. Photos by Mark Schofield, courtesy *Fine Woodworking*, © The Taunton Press, Inc. except photo on p. 10 by Rodney Diaz and photos on p.16 by Michael Pekovich, courtesy *Fine Woodworking*, © The Taunton Press, Inc.; Drawings courtesy *Fine Woodworking*, © The Taunton Press, Inc.

p. 18: An Elegant Jewelry by Strother Purdy, issue 150. Photos by William Duckworth, courtesy *Fine Woodworking*, © The Taunton Press, Inc. except photo on p. 18 by Erika Marks, courtesy *Fine Woodworking*, © The Taunton Press, Inc.; Drawings courtesy *Fine Woodworking*, © The Taunton Press, Inc.

p. 25: Shaker Oval Boxes by John Wilson, issue 102. Photos by Charley Robinson, courtesy *Fine Woodworking*, © The Taunton Press, Inc. except the photo on p. 25 by Susan Kahn, courtesy *Fine Woodworking*, © The Taunton Press, Inc.; Drawings courtesy *Fine Woodworking*, © The Taunton Press, Inc.

p. 32: Building a Humidor by Rick Allyn, issue 127. Photos by Strother Purdy, courtesy *Fine Woodworking*, © The Taunton Press, Inc.; Drawings courtesy *Fine Woodworking*, © The Taunton Press, Inc.

p. 40: Thomas Jefferson's Writing Desk by Lon Schleining, issue 144. Photos by Matthew Teague, courtesy *Fine Woodworking*, © The Taunton Press, Inc. except photo on p. 41 and 45 by Michael Pekovich, courtesy *Fine Woodworking*, © The Taunton Press, Inc.; Drawings courtesy *Fine Woodworking*, © The Taunton Press, Inc.

p. 50: Splined Miters Join Mirror Frame by Bob Gleason, issue 98. Photos by Karl Backus, courtesy *Fine Woodworking*, © The Taunton Press, Inc.; Drawings, courtesy *Fine Woodworking*, © The Taunton Press, Inc.

p. 53: Picture-Framing Techniques by Leon Segal, issue 104. Photos by Sloan Howard, courtesy *Fine Woodworking*, © The Taunton Press, Inc. except photos on p. 55 (top) and 58 by Alec Waters, courtesy *Fine Woodworking*, © The Taunton Press, Inc.; Drawings courtesy *Fine Woodworking*, © The Taunton Press, Inc.

p. 59: A Basic Mirror Frame Detailed to Your Liking by D. Douglas Mooberry, issue 128. Photos by Anatole Burkin, courtesy *Fine Woodworking*, © The Taunton Press, Inc.; Drawings courtesy *Fine Woodworking*, © The Taunton Press, Inc.

p. 64: Pear Mantle Clock by Mario Rodriguez, issue 123. Photos by Vincent Laurence, courtesy *Fine Woodworking*, © The Taunton Press, Inc. except photo on p. 64 by Scott Phillips, courtesy *Fine Woodworking*, © The Taunton Press, Inc.; Drawings courtesy *Fine Woodworking*, © The Taunton Press, Inc.

p. 72: Building a Shaker Wall Clock by Chris Becksvoort, issue 157. Photos by Erika Marks, courtesy *Fine Woodworking*, © The Taunton Press, Inc.; Drawings courtesy *Fine Woodworking*, © The Taunton Press, Inc.

p. 79: Build a Wall Shelf by Peter Turner, issue 129. Photos by Anatole Burkin, courtesy *Fine Woodworking*, © The Taunton Press, Inc. except photo on p. 79 by Michael Pekovich, courtesy *Fine Woodworking*, © The Taunton Press, Inc.; Drawings courtesy *Fine Woodworking*, © The Taunton Press, Inc.

p. 83: Colonial Cupboard by Mike Dunbar, issue 151. Photos by Asa Christiana, courtesy *Fine Woodworking*, © The Taunton Press, Inc. except photo on p. 83 by Michael Pekovich, courtesy *Fine Woodworking*, © The Taunton Press, Inc.; Drawings courtesy *Fine Woodworking*, © The Taunton Press, Inc.

p. 94: Craftsman Wall Cabinet by Ian Ingersoll, issue 140. Photos by Matthew Teague, courtesy *Fine Woodworking*, © The Taunton Press, Inc. except photos on p. 94 by Michael Pekovich, courtesy *Fine Woodworking*, © The Taunton Press, Inc; Drawings *Fine Woodworking*, © The Taunton Press, Inc.

p. 100: Magazine Cabinet by Chis Gochnour, issue 146. Photos by Anatole Burkin, courtesy *Fine Woodworking*, © The Taunton Press, Inc. except photo on p. 100 by Michael Pekovich, courtesy *Fine Woodworking*, © The Taunton Press, Inc.; Drawings courtesy *Fine Woodworking*, © The Taunton Press, Inc.

p. 108: Wineglass Cabinet by Scott Gibson, issue 158. Photos by Tim Sams, courtesy *Fine Woodworking*, © The Taunton Press, Inc.; Drawings courtesy *Fine Woodworking*, © The Taunton Press, Inc.

p. 116: Building a Shaker Round Stand by Chris Becksvoort, issue 110. Photos by Charley Robinson, courtesy *Fine Woodworking*, © The Taunton Press, Inc. except photo on p. 116 by Robert Marsala, courtesy *Fine Woodworking*, © The Taunton Press, Inc.; Drawings courtesy *Fine Woodworking*, © The Taunton Press, Inc.

p. 122: Making an End Table by Stephen Lamont, issue 120. Photos by Vincent Laurence, courtesy *Fine Woodworking*, © The Taunton Press, Inc.; Drawings courtesy *Fine Woodworking*, © The Taunton Press, Inc.

p. 131: A Sturdy Footstool by Mario Rodriguez, issue 154. Photos by Asa Christiana, courtesy *Fine Woodworking*, © The Taunton Press, Inc.; Drawings courtesy *Fine Woodworking*, © The Taunton Press, Inc.

p.139: Oval Chippendale Stool by Randall O'Donnell, issue 135. Photos by Dennis Preston, courtesy *Fine Woodworking*, © The Taunton Press, Inc. except photo on p. 139 (bottom) by Michael Pekovich, courtesy *Fine Woodworking*, © The Taunton Press, Inc.; Drawings courtesy *Fine Woodworking*, © The Taunton Press, Inc.

Index

The New Best of Fine Woodworking series

A collection of the best articles from the last ten years of Fine Woodworking.

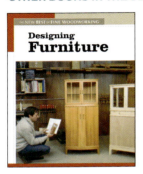

Designing Furniture
The New Best of
Fine Woodworking
From the editors of FWW
ISBN 1-56158-684-6
Product #070767
$17.95

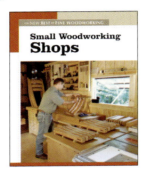

Small Woodworking Shops
The New Best of
Fine Woodworking
From the editors of FWW
ISBN 1-56158-686-2
Product #070768
$17.95

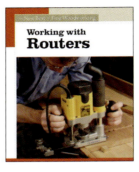

Working with Routers
The New Best of
Fine Woodworking
From the editors of FWW
ISBN 1-56158-685-4
Product #070769
$17.95

The New Best of Fine Woodworking Slipcase Set Volume 1

Designing Furniture
Working with Routers
Small Woodworking Shops
Designing and Building Cabinets
Building Small Projects
Traditional Finishing Techniques

From the editors of FWW
ISBN 1-56158-736-2
Product #070808
$85.00

Traditional Finishing Techniques
The New Best of
Fine Woodworking
From the editors of FWW
1-56158-733-8
070793
$17.95

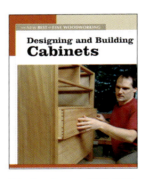

Designing and Building Cabinets
The New Best of
Fine Woodworking
From the editors of FWW
1-56158-732-X
070792
$17.95